OECD Rural Studies

Unlocking Rural Innovation

This document, as well as any data and map included herein, are without prejudice to the status of or sovereignty over any territory, to the delimitation of international frontiers and boundaries and to the name of any territory, city or area.

Please cite this publication as:
OECD (2022), *Unlocking Rural Innovation*, OECD Rural Studies, OECD Publishing, Paris, https://doi.org/10.1787/9044a961-en.

ISBN 978-92-64-59908-6 (print)
ISBN 978-92-64-61214-3 (pdf)
ISBN 978-92-64-96515-7 (HTML)
ISBN 978-92-64-85675-2 (epub)

OECD Rural Studies
ISSN 2707-3416 (print)
ISSN 2707-3424 (online)

Foreword

With OECD countries in the midst of a slowdown in trend productivity growth, coupled with the challenges of a number of megatrends and global shocks, unlocking innovation has become more important than ever. This is especially important in rural places, where innovation creation and uptake lags behind metropolitan areas, weighing down on aggregate productivity, income levels and overall well-being.

Understanding potential barriers to innovation in rural areas as well as the determinants that allow it to flourish is a critical step to fully mobilise their growth potential, and, more generally, also addresses growing gaps between rural and urban places that are contributing to geographies of discontent. Recent global shocks from the COVID-19 pandemic and Russia's large-scale aggression against Ukraine have further aggravated these gaps heightening the need for action to address them, and in particular actions that go beyond the narrow focus on science and technology. Supporting entrepreneurship, and social innovators, including tackling barriers that hold them back, is critical. These efforts need to go hand in hand with place-based policies.

The OECD, through the Regional Development Policy Committee and its Working Party for Rural Policy, has created a programme of work focusing on fostering innovation in rural regions, building on over 2 decades of policy and economic analytical experience. This publication, *Unlocking Rural Innovation,* elaborated as part of the project on Enhancing Innovation in Rural Regions, focuses on overarching messages derived from desk research, quantitative analysis and case studies in Canada, Japan, Scotland (UK), Switzerland, and the United States. It provides insights on the challenges and drivers of innovators and entrepreneurs in rural places.

Acknowledgements

This publication was produced in the OECD Centre for Entrepreneurship, SMEs, Regions and Cities (CFE), led by Lamia Kamal-Chaoui, Director, as part of the programme of work of the Regional Development Policy Committee (RDPC). This report was prepared by the Regional Development and Multi-level Governance Division of the OECD, headed by Dorothée Allain-Duprè. The process that led to the final version of this publication was under the guidance of Nadim Ahmad, Deputy Director of CFE. It was co-ordinated by Michelle Marshalian and was approved by the Regional Development Policy Committee.

The report was drafted by Michelle Marshalian. It benefited significantly from the guidance of Dorothée Allain-Duprè, Head of RDG, and Jose Enrique Garcilazo, Deputy Head of RDG. The report greatly benefited from intellectual contributions from other OECD Secretariat members, including Paolo Veneri, Alexandre Lembcke and Philip Chan (CFE), and the project's academic and business advisory committees.

Special thanks are due to members of the business and academic advisory committees listed below.

The business advisory committee is consisted of Charlotte Baylac and Asinetta Serban (Amazon Web Services); Roxanne Varza (Station F); Matt Dunne (Center on Rural Innovation); Alastair Dobson (Arran Dairies & Scottish Manufacturing Advisory Board); Jon Erni (Miaengiadina); Genero Cruz (GSMA); Shugo Yanaka (INSPIRE); Daniel Heery (Cybermoor); Nicholas Haan (Singularity University); Amin Toufani (T-labs) ; Maurizio Rossi (H-farm); Cristina Falcone (UPS); Didzis Dejus (Baltic 3D); Oliver Oram (Chainvine); Marie Gagne (Synchronex); Lyron Bentovim (Glimpes Groupe); Jane Craigie (Rural Youth Project); Ikka Nykänen (Bussiness Joenssu); Niklas Johansson (LKAB); Angel Melguizo (Directtvla and AT&T); Teresa Kittridge (100 rural women) Dr Gianluca Giuliani (Flury-Giuliani); Doug Jones (Ignite Atlantic); Zita Cobb (Shorefast); and Juan Campillo Alonso (Telefonica).

The academic advisory committee is consisted of Mikitaro Shobayashi (Gakushuin Women's University); Dr Roland Scherer (University of St. Gallen); Dr Gianluca Giuliani (Flury-Giuliani); Tim Wojan (National Science Foundation); Timothy Destefano (Harvard Business School); Ian McCoull (Scottish Enterprise); Riccardo Crescenzi (London School of Economics); Philip McCann (Sheffield University); Andres Rodriquez-Pose (London School of Economics); Ufuk Akcigit (University of Chicago); Stephen Roper (Warwick Business School); Wendy Cukier (Ryerson University Diversity Institute); Bill Maloney (World Bank); Slavo Radosevic (University College London); Heike Mayer (Bern University); Ray Bollman (Brandon University); Eveline van Leeuwen (Wageningen); Aleid Brouwer (University of Groningen); Atsuko Okudo (International Telecommunications Union); and Diane Coyle (University of Cambridge).

Ms. Jeanette Duboys prepared the report for publication, and a special thanks to Nikki Trutter, François Iglesias and Pilar Philip for editorial support.

Table of contents

FIGURES

TABLES

BOXES

Follow OECD Publications on:

http://twitter.com/OECD_Pubs

http://www.facebook.com/OECDPublications

http://www.linkedin.com/groups/OECD-Publications-4645871

http://www.youtube.com/oecdilibrary

http://www.oecd.org/oecddirect/

Abbreviations and acronyms

CIS	Community Innovation Survey
FUA	Functional Urban Areas
MR-L	Large metropolitan region
MR-M	Medium-sized metropolitan region
NMR-M	Non-Metropolitan region with access to large metropolitan region
NMR-S	Non-Metropolitan region with access to small or medium city
NMR-R	Non-Metropolitan remote region
NESTI	National Experts on Science and Technology Indicators
R&D	Research and Development
SME	Small and Medium-sized Enterprise
STI	Science, Technology and Innovation
TL2	OECD Territorial Level 2 (large regions)
TL3	OECD Territorial Level 3 (small regions)

Executive summary

OECD countries are currently in the midst of a global slowdown regarding innovation, in particular ground-breaking, productivity-inducing innovations, as witnessed by widespread anaemic productivity growth (OECD, 2019[1]). Lower productivity growth translates into lower long-term economic growth and, in turn, lower wages and well-being. This is why actions to drive innovation – a precursor of productivity growth (Aghion and Howitt, 1990[2]; OECD, 2016[3]; Romer, 1990[4]) – are so important. Those actions are particularly important for rural regions. Across large OECD regions (TL2) in European countries, high-technology (high-tech) innovation is associated with a five times higher increase in jobs when regions have larger shares of people living in non-metropolitan regions, as compared to those in more metropolitan regions.

To support and boost rural innovation, this report, the first of a series focusing on enhancing rural innovation, considers the following elements:

- The nature of innovation in rural regions.
- The framework conditions for encouraging innovative entrepreneurship, in particular among young entrepreneurs.
- Measuring the impact of innovation in rural regions.

Understanding innovation in rural regions

How we measure innovation matters

It is important to understand how innovation occurs in rural regions before measuring it. While innovation is officially defined through the Oslo Manual as "a new or improved product or process that has been made available to potential users (product) or brought into use by the unit (process)" (OECD/Eurostat, 2018[5]), in practice, many governments only consider innovation in the context of science and technology requiring heavy research and development (R&D) investments or patents. This is problematic as this is only one form of innovation. Other forms involving new or significantly improved types of production and processes, business models or those that are not primarily profit-driven, are often overlooked. Regional governments in particular, often take a broader view, embodying entrepreneurship and start-up activities in notions of innovation, as opposed to the narrower focus on science- and technology-based innovations that are often supported through R&D grants and tax benefits.

This matters because a simplistic look at innovation through a narrow lens may suggest that rural areas are innately less innovative. However, evidence from in-depth studies suggests otherwise. For example, analysis in Scotland (United Kingdom), where our research takes a broader view of innovation, suggests that differences in innovation across geographies reflect differences in economic structures (size and age of firms). Even with a narrower science, technology and innovation (STI) view of innovation, differences seem to reflect sectoral specialisations. For example, in the United States, adjusting for the share of occupations that are involved in patenting (of high-tech innovation) reduces disparities in patenting activity between metropolitan and non-metropolitan regions by a factor of 75. Furthermore, some evidence suggests that aspects of rural areas, such as gaps in access to basic services and markets, often compel rural entrepreneurs to be more innovative (Shearmu, Carrincazeaux and Doloreux, 2016[6]; Simonen and McCann, 2008[7]; Simonen and McCann, 2010[8]). The report proposes several indicators to consider jointly and caveats to consider when doing so.

Governments need to look beyond the STI framework in rural regions

The hypothesis that rural areas are typically centres of low innovation seems to be a construct of the definition used to measure innovation. The broader notion of innovation for rural regions requires consideration of product, process, public and social innovations. In doing so, resources for innovation are (re)directed towards the types of innovations that matter and that can boost welfare and productivity in rural regions.

Reducing barriers to innovative entrepreneurship is a priority in rural regions

Entrepreneurs in rural regions face significant challenges with respect to access to basic framework conditions for innovation

Building a level playing field for entrepreneurs in rural regions means reflecting on place-based challenges such as government capacity, costs of services or local regulations that may hinder the effective implementation of policies in rural regions.

Governments need to address barriers to key framework conditions such as unequal access to education and digital infrastructure

A focus on innovation processes that are more common in rural areas also requires a focus on framework conditions, such as early-stage education for entrepreneurs and enabling local authorities to create incentives for increasing deployment and affordability of digital infrastructure.

Young entrepreneurs in rural regions are at a disadvantage

There is a strong relationship between entrepreneurship and broader notions of innovation. However, youth start-ups are lagging in rural areas. In 2019, there were proportionately 25% fewer young start-up entrepreneurs in rural areas as compared to cities, according to the analysis from the European Union Labour Force Survey (EU-LFS) on 26 European OECD countries (2011 and 2019). Furthermore, young entrepreneurs living in rural areas, towns and suburbs are close to 30% less likely to be in training one year prior to starting the firm as compared to those in cities. Moreover, when they do start a firm, these young start-up entrepreneurs in rural areas, towns and suburbs tend to be more educated than their counterparts in cities, pointing to the significant untapped entrepreneurial potential of lower-educated groups in rural areas.

Social entrepreneurship and innovation have room to play a strong role in bringing innovation and opportunities to rural regions

Where there are gaps in public services, access to government services and support in the entrepreneurial ecosystem, social entrepreneurs and innovation can be important stimuli to fill those gaps. Social innovation is innovation with a social purpose. It "can concern conceptual, process or product change, organisational change and changes in financing, and can deal with new relationships with stakeholders and territories" (OECD, forthcoming[9]). However, a lack of acknowledgement of the critical role of social entrepreneurs, in some cases, an enabling legal framework and resource constraints are often hindering social innovators from fulfilling this role.

References

Aghion, P. and P. Howitt (1990), "A model of growth through creative destruction", *National Bureau of Economic Research*, Vol. w3223. [2]

OECD (2019), *OECD Economic Outlook, Volume 2019 Issue 1*, OECD Publishing, Paris, https://doi.org/10.1787/b2e897b0-en. [1]

OECD (2016), *OECD Regional Outlook 2016: Productive Regions for Inclusive Societies*, OECD Publishing, Paris, https://doi.org/10.1787/9789264260245-en. [3]

OECD (forthcoming), *Enhancing Innovation in Rural Regions: Scotland (UK)*, OECD Publishing, Paris. [9]

OECD/Eurostat (2018), *Oslo Manual 2018: Guidelines for Collecting, Reporting and Using Data on Innovation, 4th Edition*, The Measurement of Scientific, Technological and Innovation Activities, OECD Publishing, Paris/Eurostat, Luxembourg, https://doi.org/10.1787/9789264304604-en. [5]

Romer, P. (1990), "Endogenous technological change", *Journal of Political Economy*, Vol. 98/5 (part 2), pp. S71-S102, https://www.jstor.org/stable/2937632. [4]

Shearmu, R., C. Carrincazeaux and D. Doloreux (2016), *Handbook on the Geographies of Innovation*, Edward Elgar Publishing, https://doi.org/10.4337/9781784710774. [6]

Simonen, J. and P. McCann (2010), "Knowledge transfers and innovation: The role of labour markets and R&D co-operation between agents and institutions", *Papers in Regional Science*, Vol. 89/2, pp. 295-309, https://doi.org/10.1111/j.1435-5957.2010.00299.x. [8]

Simonen, J. and P. McCann (2008), "Firm innovation: The influence of R&D cooperation and the geography of human capital inputs", *Journal of Urban Economics*, Vol. 64/1, pp. 146-154, https://doi.org/10.1016/j.jue.2007.10.002. [7]

1 Assessments and recommendations

OECD countries today are facing a global slump in innovation, with fewer innovations that radically change the way our society works and a concurrent productivity slowdown. This slowdown is affecting countries across the globe, impacting wages, well-being and economic opportunities (OECD, 2019[1]).

Yet innovation is a precursor of long-term growth and productivity (Aghion and Howitt, 1990[2]; OECD, 2016[3]; Romer, 1990[4]). Across large OECD regions (TL2[1]), high-technology (high-tech) innovation[2] has five times more impact on jobs in regions with larger shares of people living in non-metropolitan regions.[3]

Innovation can bring well-being to people and places, yet it is important to understand that its impact varies across territories. A one-unit increase in patent intensity is associated with a 91% increase in productivity in regions with a relatively high share of non-metropolitan population, against a 54% increase in regions with a relatively lower share of non-metropolitan population in European OECD countries. This also translates into differences in average household income. Increased patent intensity is associated with an 86% increase in household income for those regions with a relatively high share of non-metropolitan population but only 30% in regions with a relatively smaller non-metropolitan population.

Welfare-inducing innovation is not automatic – especially in rural regions. Often regions with dependency on fewer sectors and fragile access to basic framework conditions have a harder time adapting to changes induced by innovation. Higher average household income associated with patent intensity will also raise wage inequality[4] and the increase is higher in rural places. A one-unit increase in patent intensity is associated with 11% higher inequality in regions with a higher share of non-metropolitan population, against a 3% increase in areas with a lower share of non-metropolitan population.

There are significant and growing gaps in innovation and productivity between metro[5] and non-metropolitan regions, meaning that many rural areas can potentially be less resilient to shocks and structural changes brought on by megatrends. Indeed, since the economic shock of the 2008 global financial crisis, non-metro areas have shown higher vulnerability to shock increasing their gaps in gross domestic product (GDP) per capita with respect to metro regions. Furthermore, rural regions must address demographic challenges associated with higher rates of population decline and ageing, which are having disproportionate impacts on rural communities.

Traditionally, subsidies have been one of the primary mechanisms through which many governments have addressed such challenges. However, there are substantial concerns related to the short-term impact of such subsidies and an increasing awareness that such efforts do not produce long-lasting effects. Unlocking rural innovation can mitigate the growing gaps and unlock new opportunities, especially related to digital and green transitions.

Importantly, governments should take advantage of the full benefits of innovation in a broader sense, as opposed to the narrower science, technology and innovation (STI) approach to rural innovation. There is significant potential to boost productivity growth by creating place-based policies to encourage broader entrepreneurial innovations in rural regions with less mature markets. For instance, in related studies in Scotland (United Kingdom), Switzerland and the United States, productivity growth is still strong in non-metropolitan areas and regions, against a slowdown present in urban areas over the last decade. Indeed, the majority of productivity growth in non-metropolitan areas has reflected upgrading current processes and products (OECD, forthcoming[5]; forthcoming[6]).

Understanding rural innovation

Unlocking rural innovation is crucial to addressing these challenges and indeed taking advantage of the potential benefits of digitalisation and technological change to maintain and boost well-being standards. But to unlock rural innovation, we need to understand how individuals innovate and adopt innovations in rural places. Once we have a clear vision of innovation in rural places, we can start creating the right framework conditions and innovation-enabling environments for individuals and entrepreneurs.

The importance of defining innovation through a rural lens

The Oslo Manual defines innovation as "a new or improved product or process (or combination thereof) […] that has been made available to potential users (product) or brought into use by the unit (process)" (OECD/Eurostat, 2018[7]). However, many governments consider innovation *only or primarily* related to science and technology, focusing policies and programmes primarily on research and development (R&D) investments or patents. This is only one form of innovation that is often associated with specific sectors and occupations. In contrast, innovation in rural places tends to happen on a broader base, which includes significantly improved or new types of production and processes, business models or innovations that are not uniquely profit-driven (such as social as well as public innovation). These are often overlooked by standard policies and programmes for innovation.

Defining innovation narrowly as STI limits market forces. Governments, enacting policies that are ill-defined for rural places are missing out on their growth potential. In turn, this can hinder factors of productivity growth that may interact with macro-factors and structural reforms. Building the conditions for innovation and productivity that consider opportunities and barriers across the different territories will ensure that the mechanisms underlying productivity growth are well targeted. For this purpose, the report identifies several alternative indicators associated with innovation to be considered jointly and caveats to be made when they are being used.

For instance, cities benefit from economies of agglomeration as well as a diversified industrial base, including high value-added activities. Policies focused on encouraging innovation in cities are tied to indicators related to the flow of goods, services and skills and increasing competition that drive forces for innovation, in particular among large, incumbent firms. In contrast, rural areas have less industrial diversification and fewer incumbents across all sectors, including agriculture and manufacturing. Among other goods, rural places depend on tradeable goods that can be exported to cities and other markets. As rural economies transition to service industries and, increasingly, digital trade and services, the relative comparative advantage of these areas will transition to the intersection of diversified services tied to nature-based comparative resources, among other sectors. In this context, innovation based on new entrepreneurial activity, process-based innovations and indicators to capture these will be crucial to ensure rural places can add more value to these activities.

Although the primary focus of this report is on non-agricultural output, it is important to note that the findings are also relevant to agricultural activities, which can often benefit from the same framework where there is significant scope for innovation. For example, in a study on block-chain, new nature-based branding and marketing in organic, fair trade, organic or net-zero production can also be considered as process and product innovations that provide means to break into new markets and bring new services to existing ones (Bianchini and Kwon, 2020[8]).

To date, there are many studies at the subnational level that focus on science and technology or regional innovation systems in metro areas and cities, but relatively few that systematically try to understand innovation in rural regions.

Entrepreneurs as drivers of innovation

Starting a firm is a good proxy for new activities in rural places. While high value-added activities are still strongly associated with agglomeration in cities, local demands and solutions for challenges in rural places create the impetus for entrepreneurs to address larger societal challenges. For rural entrepreneurs, these are not as frequently hinged on products and production processes.

Rural regions have the opportunity of developing a model of growth and innovation that benefit from local resources, assets, bottom-up solutions and new opportunities available in those areas. Rural markets allow for experimentation and incubation of ideas, due to higher market dominance of incumbents, lower risks of intellectual property leakages and low operation costs based on the resources and opportunities of the region, which is, by definition, substantially different from those in cities.

Young entrepreneurs are important drivers of innovation for rural regions. Diversity, in age, gender and cultural backgrounds tends to breed new ideas to answer old questions. Young entrepreneurs tend to adopt more recent methods for providing services and products. Such services tend to better cater to the future of the workforce across all types of territories. Encouraging opportunities for youth in rural regions has spill-over effects on the rest of the community, where depopulation and youth flight is often a primary concern.

This report, *Unlocking Rural Innovation,* is the first in a series that will systematically address the following areas:

- Better understanding how innovation unfolds in rural places and reframing how we think about rural innovation.
- Identifying framework conditions and policy levers to encourage innovative entrepreneurship.
- Measuring the impacts of innovation on rural performance and well-being standards.

Assessment

We need to overcome biases and expand beyond traditional measures of innovation in rural regions

Innovation as defined by the Oslo Manual (OECD/Eurostat, 2018[7]) encompasses non-tech-based innovations, such as innovations in business models and social innovations. For rural regions, it is important to apply this broader definition of innovation that encompasses new activities, new products and new processes, regardless of whether they involve high-tech activities.

It is increasingly important to rural-proof how we measure innovation in rural regions in order to better design place-based policies for rural regions. For example, patents, as a common proxy for innovation, lack the capacity to account for the occupational and sectoral structure of rural regions. Quite often, this can bias how we understand innovation, primarily in high-tech industry. It easily overlooks innovations in process and non-technical innovations that are more relevant for rural regions. Rural-proofing or viewing statistics and analysis through a rural lens can help by:

1. Adjusting pre-existing indicators to address the underlying occupational, sectoral and territorial structure of rural places.

2. Expanding beyond the traditional science and technology as indicators of innovation in rural regions.

This report proposes measuring innovation in rural regions using a variety of tools, each carrying advantages and disadvantages. These potential measures include, for example:

- Self-reported innovation measures on introducing new products or processes to the firm or market (with a large enough sample size).
- Product-level data that demonstrate upgrading (especially for the manufacturing and tradeable sectors).
- R&D jobs and investment (focused on relevant sectors).
- Adjusted patent intensity (accounting for industry and occupational structure of territories).
- Proxies for absorptive capacity such as shares of high-growth firms and productivity, start-up rates, especially among young entrepreneurs.

In addition to defining innovation, defining rural areas has an impact on how rural innovation is perceived. Rural and non-metropolitan regions are very diverse: some are close to metropolitan regions; others are close the intermediate cities and others are remote. Each type of region requires a differentiated focus.

As such, the framework for enhancing innovation in rural regions is built on the understanding that it is important to: i) take a broad view of innovation, one more closely adapted to leveraging the full potential of rural regions; ii) ensure that rural regions have the appropriate framework conditions to unlock rural innovation which includes labour, physical and digital markets, access to finance and government services; iii) specifically encourage networks and linkages through the free flow of individuals, goods and firm activities across regions.

Innovation, and its adoption, is a function of skills and capital, yet little is known about how to support individuals as drivers of entrepreneurship in rural regions

A few framework conditions particularly matter in terms of innovation. Innovation, and its adoption, is a function of skills, capital and investment (Autor, 2014[9]; Solow, 1957[10]). Framework policies regulating markets, competition, finance and human capital endowments are important factors for encouraging innovation (Aghion et al., 2001[11]; Andersson et al., 2009[12]; Bloom, Draca and Van Reenen, 2016[13]; Goos, Manning and Salomons, 2014[14]; Grossman and Helpman, 1990[15]). However, most of the analysis and research on framework conditions for innovation overlooks regional differences, especially for rural regions. For example, competition may well be a driver of growth in regions with large firms and high levels of investment, but an advantage of rural innovation is a less stifling environment that allows "slow innovation" to take place.

Part of the challenge in understanding rural innovation is access to data and appropriate monitoring and evaluation mechanisms. In addition, there is also a challenge related to building capacity in understanding, monitoring and evaluating rural innovation and developing initiatives. Governments have a myriad of policy tools to help offset the growing divide in education and access to capital and investments that hinder rural innovation; however, such policies are often inadvertently misguided if they are territorially blind and overly sector-focused.

Better indicators can give us a more accurate picture of innovation in rural areas

Analysing innovation through a rural lens provides a more promising and nuanced picture of innovation in rural regions. For example, in Canada, the share of occupations with a high patent potential is no longer only located in the coastal regions. In studies associated with this report, evidence from Switzerland suggests that R&D investments are associated with more jobs and inward expenditure in rural regions than in metropolitan areas. For example, in 2019, close to 35 cents per Swiss franc spent on R&D were outsourced; in rural regions, only 4 cents per Swiss franc left the firm for R&D expenses (OECD, 2021[16]).

Innovators innovate no matter where they are located. When looking at the narrower view of innovation, differences seem to reflect firm and territorial characteristics such as occupational or sectoral specialisations. For example, in the United States, adjusting for the share of occupations that are involved in patenting (of high-tech innovation) reduces disparities in patenting activity between metropolitan and non-metropolitan regions by a factor of 75. Evidence from an innovation-based survey in Scotland (United Kingdom) finds that controlling for sector and firm-level attributes, rural and urban entrepreneurs innovate at the same rate. Geography, in itself, is not the only determinant of who innovates: differences are driven by firm characteristics across places, for example, the size and age of businesses that increase the likelihood of innovation. In Scotland, large firms (101 or more employees) are 28% more likely to innovate than smaller ones, while young firms (0-5 years old) are 22% more likely to innovate than older ones. However, in rural areas and towns in Scotland, there is a much lower share of large and a relatively higher share of older firms.

While innovators are the same across regions, the return to innovation is larger in rural regions. In Scotland and the United States, both the reallocation of resources and the upskilling and upgrading of pre-existing resources in accessible rural and remote rural regions still contribute positively to productivity growth despite the fact that there is allocative inefficiency (OECD, forthcoming[5]; forthcoming[6]).

Entrepreneurs are drivers of innovation

High business dynamics are an important determinant of innovation and the resilience of regions. Overall, however, there is less dynamism in firms rural areas, with lower birth and death rates. There are 13% more firms created per 1 000 workers in urban regions as compared to rural regions, and a 9% lower rate of firm closure. Building a dynamic environment with low entry barriers and fast business exits brings opportunities for change in the business environment for rural regions.

Second, the sectoral composition of rural regions is different. Growing sectors in rural and intermediate areas tend to be in industry, hospitality and construction. Close to 60% of industry is located in rural and intermediate areas, while 50% of hospitality is also located in intermediate and rural areas. Likewise, the importance of the agricultural sector is strong in rural regions, despite growing service sectors.

Young and new entrepreneurs are important to rural regions and are often associated with innovation; yet they are still lagging in rural areas. In European rural areas, for example, there are 2 missing young start-up entrepreneurs per 1 000 inhabitants – that is 25% fewer young start-up entrepreneurs in rural areas than in cities. In 2011-19, a relative and absolute fall in the number of young founders in rural areas has outpaced peers in cities, suburbs and towns.

Young entrepreneurs as an age group are particularly important for encouraging innovation. With demographic change and ageing rural regions, the importance of finding attractive opportunities for those areas is increasingly important. In European OECD countries, young rural entrepreneurs, however, are 8.6% less likely to start a company than those in cities. Most of this difference is explained by socio-economic characteristics such as education, sector of activity, household characteristics and living conditions.

There are specific differences in the conditions in which young prospective entrepreneurs operate. In particular, young women in rural areas as well as towns and suburbs are 7.5% less likely to start a firm than young male in rural areas. Young entrepreneurs in cities have a 57% likelihood of having received training the year prior to starting a firm, while those in rural areas, towns and suburbs were only 26% to have received training in the year prior to starting a firm.

Young rural entrepreneurs are not inherently different from entrepreneurs in other areas; however, they have limited access to educational and government resources that hinder their potential. Providing access to create a level playing field is a start. However, building curricula tied to local opportunities and focusing on vocational skills is critical for the future of young rural entrepreneurs. In addition, more is needed to level the playing field for young female entrepreneurs in rural areas and help unlock rural innovation.

Access to education and skills upgrading opportunities is an important driver of entrepreneurship among young start-up entrepreneurs. Reducing socio-economic disparities – such as access to training, education, and employment opportunities (sector and occupation), and proxies for household income, education and migration status – has the potential of reducing the potential start-up rates by half. There is also room to improve framework conditions in regions, for example, access to digital infrastructure and export markets.

Building the case for social innovation

Social innovation and entrepreneurship can bring important opportunities for rural regions and individual well-being. With a primary purpose that goes beyond profit maximisation, social entrepreneurs and innovators can provide services to rural communities that have often been left behind in rural regions. Community anchor organisations can support the public sector in creating a vision for the community, while social innovators and entrepreneurs often can only operate if their service is of need to the community.

Recommendations and takeaways

This report identifies a number of recommendations and takeaways to help unlock the innovation potential of rural regions by rebuilding the scope of policies and programmes for innovation by:

- Going beyond science and technology as indicators of innovation in rural regions.
- Recognising the strong correlation between entrepreneurship and innovation, especially youth with entrepreneurship.
- Targeting barriers such as limited access to improving skills and government resources that hinder the potential for rural entrepreneurs.
- Building evidence and programmes to support the demographics in rural regions, such as older workers and women.
- Unlocking barriers, such as legal status and access to funding and resources, for social innovators and entrepreneurs, as an important stimulus for well-being-focused innovation in rural regions.
- Understanding that while innovation is positively associated with increasing incomes and employment in rural regions, without place-based policies, it will also increase inequalities, in part due to innovation-induced structural change.

References

Aghion, P. et al. (2001), "Competition, imitation and growth with step-by-step innovation", *Review of Economic Studies*, Vol. 68/3, pp. 467-492, https://doi.org/10.1111/1467-937x.00177. [11]

Aghion, P. and P. Howitt (1990), "A model of growth through creative destruction", *National Bureau of Economic Research*, Vol. w3223. [2]

Andersson, F. et al. (2009), "Reaching for the stars: Who pays for talent in innovative industries?", *The Economic Journal*, Vol. 119/538, pp. F308-F332, https://doi.org/10.1111/j.1468-0297.2009.02277.x. [12]

Autor, D. (2014), "Polanyi's Paradox and the shape of employment growth", National Bureau of Economic Research, Cambridge, MA, https://doi.org/10.3386/w20485. [9]

Bianchini, M. and I. Kwon (2020), "Blockchain for SMEs and entrepreneurs in Italy", *OECD SME and Entrepreneurship Papers*, Vol. 20, https://www.oecd.org/cfe/smes/Blockchain%20for%20SMEs%20in%20Italy.pdf. [8]

Bloom, N., M. Draca and J. Van Reenen (2016), "Trade induced technical change? The impact of Chinese imports on innovation, IT and productivity", *The Review of Economic Studies*, Vol. 83/1, pp. 87-117. [13]

Goos, M., A. Manning and A. Salomons (2014), "Explaining Job Polarization: Routine-Biased Technological Change and Offshoring", *American Economic Review*, Vol. 104/8, pp. 2509-2526, https://doi.org/10.1257/aer.104.8.2509. [14]

Grossman, G. and E. Helpman (1990), "Trade, innovation, and growth", *The American Economic Review*, Vol. 80/2, pp. 86-91, http://www.jstor.org/stable/2006548 (accessed on 9 November 2020). [15]

OECD (2021), "Building local ecosystems for social innovation: A methodological framework", *OECD Local Economic and Employment Development (LEED) Papers*, No. 2021/06, OECD Publishing, Paris, https://doi.org/10.1787/bef867cd-en. [16]

OECD (2019), *OECD Economic Outlook, Volume 2019 Issue 1*, OECD Publishing, Paris, https://doi.org/10.1787/b2e897b0-en. [1]

OECD (2016), *OECD Regional Outlook 2016: Productive Regions for Inclusive Societies*, OECD Publishing, Paris, https://doi.org/10.1787/9789264260245-en. [3]

OECD (forthcoming), *Enhancing Innovation in Rural Regions: Scotland (UK)*, OECD Publishing, Paris. [5]

OECD (forthcoming), *Enhancing Innovation in Rural Regions: Switzerland*, OECD Publishing, Paris. [6]

OECD/Eurostat (2018), *Oslo Manual 2018: Guidelines for Collecting, Reporting and Using Data on Innovation, 4th Edition*, The Measurement of Scientific, Technological and Innovation Activities, OECD Publishing, Paris/Eurostat, Luxembourg, https://doi.org/10.1787/9789264304604-en. [7]

Romer, P. (1990), "Endogenous technological change", *Journal of Political Economy*, Vol. 98/5 (part 2), pp. S71-S102, https://www.jstor.org/stable/2937632. [4]

Solow, R. (1957), "Technical change and the aggregate production function", *The Review of Economics and Statistics*, pp. 312-320. [10]

Notes

[1] OECD large (TL2) regions represent the first administrative tier of subnational government, for example, the Ontario Province in Canada. This classification is elaborated in Box 3.1 of chapter 3 of the report.

[2] This refers to patenting intensity or the number of patents over the number of people in the active labour force.

[3] This refers to individuals living within the 75 percentile of regions with the highest levels of individuals living in non-metropolitan regions. The alternative group captures the individuals within the 25th percentile of regions that have the lowest shares of individuals living in non-metropolitan regions.

[4] As measured using the Gini index which is a measure of income inequality.

[5] For all chapters of this report, "metro" refers to "metropolitan."

2 Introduction

Designing policies for innovation through a rural lens can create better opportunities for rural regions. Yet there are challenges in ensuring measurement tools are not territorially blind and can capture innovation in rural places beyond the standard science and technology indicators. Re-evaluating how we measure and evaluate innovation helps in designing place-based policies to unlock rural innovation. This report calls for better measurement tools for rural innovation and reveals the importance of young start-up entrepreneurs to unlock rural innovation and its effects on driving outcomes in rural places.

Today's rural economies are going through fundamental changes to the way people, places and firms work and interact with each other. In part, this is due to how megatrends in digitalisation, innovation, demographics[1] and the environment are changing societies. More recently, the health pandemic revealed underlying weaknesses in public service delivery and place-based policies specifically in rural regions (OECD, 2020[1]; 2021[2]). Some rural regions, with low density and large distances to urban areas, often suffer disproportionately from economic shocks and structural change. Not only do they miss out on agglomeration benefits that dense areas enjoy, they suffer from lower levels of financial resources for public goods and government programmes targeted at improving skills, and infrastructure and providing adequate public services. However, rural areas can also be important places of opportunity and a source of ingenuity (OECD, 2016[3]).

Individuals and firms innovate in fundamentally similar ways but are exposed to different challenges and contexts. Rural regions often face different economic activities and business models than those in denser areas. They also suffer disproportionately from lower access to capital, labour, infrastructure and government services.

Further distances to markets is one of the major characteristics of non-metropolitan and rural regions. This can both be an advantage and a disadvantage. In the case of export and tradable goods and services, non-metropolitan and rural economies lack dense markets. Innovation, digitalisation and new technologies have the potential to overcome barriers to transport costs and access to markets. For this reason, and many others, innovation in rural places is of crucial importance.

In rural regions, the relative lack of access to basic resources has, in some cases, been managed through local ingenuity and, notably, innovation. Innovations can, for example, overcome market distances (online services, automated delivery services, etc.), labour force training challenges (distance learning) and access to services critical to the well-functioning of framework conditions (social innovation and public sector innovation). Nonetheless, structural inequalities, preparedness for megatrends such as demographic change and globalisation, and the missed opportunities associated with innovation for growth, continue to plague rural well-being. For example, changes in the demographic composition of areas mean demands for public and private services need to transition. Changes in supply chains due to increased globalisation means new opportunities for rural entrepreneurs to innovate using new products. Instead of observing improvements in well-being, studies demonstrate growing gaps in productivity and wages and depopulation of rural regions over the past decades (OECD, 2020[1]), suggesting that rural places have not fully reaped the benefits of globalisation and digitalisation.

Many rural regions are going through population decline. When populations, especially the skilled and youth, move to more densely populated areas, rural regions often lose potential gains in productivity that are crucial to survival. The extent of productivity and brain drain varies by the various types of rural regions. Population decline in rural places also calls for productivity gains to maintain well-being standards. Instead of fighting depopulation, governments can increase opportunities by encouraging the innovative endeavours of start-ups, supporting firms adopting pre-existing innovations and encouraging upskilling of rural populations to build the conditions to support the potential of rural areas and rural innovators. Ensuring that rural areas equally benefit from innovation breakthroughs can unlock the productivity gains that help balance the flow of individuals in and out of rural areas.

Entrepreneurs and innovators all share certain entrepreneurial, risk-taking or problem-solving characteristics (Pekkala Kerr and Kerr, 2020[4]). Differences in sectoral, occupational and territorial resources impact how innovations are produced and registered and, importantly, the societal or business purpose they serve. As such, the way we think about innovation in the context of rural regions merits reflection. Baumol (1990[5]) argued that entrepreneurial innovation has two main forms, driven by formal experiments or through the combination of tacit and formal knowledge and creativity to address barriers and become commercialised. In rural regions, formal innovations driven by large firms are less common and, when they do happen, may not always be attributed to the region because of reporting biases. Instead, innovation in rural areas is driven by the action of entrepreneurs looking to overcome barriers that often serve a local or niche market. In some cases, this has also led to major technological disruptions. Innovation benefits from "systems" thinking and the formal and informal links that ensure the alignment of actors (OECD, forthcoming[6]). As will be further elaborated in this report, focusing on increasing the conditions that encourage the ecosystem around innovation and entrepreneurial activities is more relevant for rural well-being than the focus on innovation in high-technology sectors alone.

Innovation as a predecessor of rural well-being

Innovation is a precursor of long-term growth, productivity and, in some cases, well-being (Aghion and Howitt, 1990[7]; OECD, 2016[3]; Romer, 1990[8]). Enhancing the creation, adoption and diffusion of innovative products and processes,[2] is often a target of policy makers and community leaders alike. Yet, innovation can be destructive in industries that are on the decline (Autor, 2014[9]; Aghion, Antonin and Bunel, 2021[10]). They can replace human labour and jobs with machines, removing a major source of income and welfare for areas where such declining industries are geographically located (McCann, 2019[11]).

Framework conditions matter for innovation. Innovation, and its adoption, is a function of production inputs, skills, capital and investment (Autor, 2014[9]; Solow, 1957[12]). As such, governments wishing to encourage innovation-led development also target programmes that improve the general framework conditions for firms and entrepreneurs. Framework policies regulating markets, competition, finance and human capital endowments are important factors for encouraging innovation (Aghion et al., 2001[13]; Andersson et al., 2009[14]; Bloom, Draca and Van Reenen, 2016[15]; Goos, Manning and Salomons, 2014[16]; Grossman and Helpman, 1990[17]), yet the academic literature on framework conditions for innovation often overlooks regional heterogeneities and, even more so, when trying to specifically understand innovation framework conditions in rural regions.

Governments have a myriad of policy tools to help offset the growing divide; however, such policies are often inadvertently misguided if they are *territorially blind* or *geographically misdirected* (OECD, 2014[18]). Understanding how to calibrate the policy levers that trigger benefits of innovation in rural regions can contribute to the reduction of current and expected future inequalities while reducing the growing "geography of discontent" (McCann, 2019[11]; OECD, 2019[19]) that is built from territorial inequalities between metropolitan and non-metropolitan regions. These inequalities have exacerbated the vulnerability of non-metropolitan regions to shocks such as the global financial crisis, the COVID-19 health pandemic and the large-scale Russian aggression on Ukraine. For instance, with inequalities in access to health services, individuals impacted by COVID-19 were more vulnerable. Likewise, firms with limited access to government services may have not been able to benefit from relief funds as substantially as those in metropolitan regions with a strong presence of government service providers. The recent war being waged by Russia on Ukraine is also now impacting energy prices in European countries. Those regions with low-quality housing stock and lower incomes are more vulnerable to increases in energy pricing and may be more exposed to extreme weather conditions. There is substantial and growing policy literature focusing on the territorial aspects of rural and regional policymaking (EC, 2020[20]; 2020[21]; OECD, 2013[22]; 2014[18]).

Innovation diffusion and adoption often occur in networks (Akcigit, Grigsby and Nicholas, 2017[23]; Lengyel et al., 2020[24]; Sorenson, 2018[25]) and are subject to agglomeration forces and positive spill-overs that vary by territory (Ahrend et al., 2017[26]; Maloney and Valencia Caicedo, 2022[27]). As such, the diffusion and adoption of innovation are equally – if not more – important in rural regions. For individuals and entrepreneurs in less dense areas – where access to labour, capital, markets and public services can be hampered by gaps in physical and digital infrastructure policies – networks of innovation diffusion and partnerships take an increasingly central role.

Following the literature review, our current knowledge of drivers of innovation and rural development tells us that:

- Entrepreneurs and innovators are fundamentally looking to overcome challenges and search for opportunities, whether they are in rural or urban regions.
- Innovation is a predecessor of growth but not necessarily well-being for all territories.
- Framework conditions encouraging innovation and innovation adoption and diffusion can be better targeted to satisfy the economic structure of rural regions.
- Innovation diffusion and adoption occur in networks and can be a source of growth for rural areas if barriers to physical and digital distances can be addressed.

While there is a multitude of research on innovation and geography, there is no systematic study on drivers of innovation in rural regions that focuses specifically on unlocking rural innovation. Seeing innovation through a rural lens means understanding what innovation and entrepreneurship look like in rural regions, before studying how they can be improved. The current report attempts to contribute to closing this gap.

The analysis makes use of several novel sources of data and reveals a number of findings:

- Entrepreneurs innovate across all regions. Analysing innovation indicators through a rural lens can give a more accurate picture of innovation that is more relevant for rural regions. While standard indicators of innovation and patent intensity find that rural places are lagging in innovation intensity, more refined measures, that adjust for occupational composition, find a different picture. In the United States, adjusting for occupational composition reduced the disparity between metropolitan and non-metropolitan regions by 75%.
- Rural entrepreneurship and young start-up rates, important indicators of innovation, are lagging in rural areas. Young entrepreneurs need to have equal access to education and training resources in rural areas as compared to their peers in cities, towns and suburbs. They would also benefit from policies that could level other socio-economic disparities, especially those that disproportionately affect women.
- Innovation is positively associated with increasing income and employment in rural regions; however, it can also be associated with increasing wage inequalities. Working on policies that can level the playing field between territories means taking a place-based approach. In particular, for rural areas, social innovation and entrepreneurship offer solutions to challenges that the public sector has a more difficult time addressing.

This report is structured into three main sections following this introduction. The first section focuses on measuring and broadening the measurements of innovation beyond science and technologies to better capture innovation in rural places. The second section examines entrepreneurship in rural places. The last section focuses on outcomes associated with innovation.

References

Aghion, P., C. Antonin and S. Bunel (2021), *The Power of Creative Destruction*, Harvard University Press, https://doi.org/10.4159/9780674258686. [10]

Aghion, P. et al. (2001), "Competition, imitation and growth with step-by-step innovation", *Review of Economic Studies*, Vol. 68/3, pp. 467-492, https://doi.org/10.1111/1467-937x.00177. [13]

Aghion, P. and P. Howitt (1990), "A model of growth through creative destruction", *National Bureau of Economic Research*, Vol. w3223. [7]

Ahrend, R. et al. (2017), "What makes cities more productive? Evidence from five OECD countries on the role of urban governance", *Journal of Regional Science*, Vol. 57/3, pp. 385-410, https://doi.org/10.1111/jors.12334. [26]

Akcigit, U., J. Grigsby and T. Nicholas (2017), "The rise of American ingenuity: Innovation and inventors of the golden age", No. w23047, National Bureau of Economic Research. [23]

Andersson, F. et al. (2009), "Reaching for the stars: Who pays for talent in innovative industries?", *The Economic Journal*, Vol. 119/538, pp. F308-F332, https://doi.org/10.1111/j.1468-0297.2009.02277.x. [14]

Autor, D. (2014), *Polanyi's Paradox and the Shape of Employment Growth*, National Bureau of Economic Research, Cambridge, MA, https://doi.org/10.3386/w20485. [9]

Baumol, W. (1990), "Entrepreneurship: Productive, unproductive, and destructive", *Journal of Political Economy*, Vol. 98/5, pp. 893–921, https://www.jstor.org/stable/2937617. [5]

Bloom, N., M. Draca and J. Van Reenen (2016), "Trade induced technical change? The impact of Chinese imports on innovation, IT and productivity", *The Review of Economic Studies*, Vol. 83/1, pp. 87-117. [15]

EC (2020), *Enhancing Rural Innovation*, European Commission, https://research-and-innovation.ec.europa.eu/research-area/agriculture-forestry-and-rural-areas/enhancing-rural-innovation_en (accessed on 8 March 2020). [20]

EC (2020), *Regional Innovation Monitor Plus*, European Commission, https://research-and-innovation.ec.europa.eu/statistics/performance-indicators/regional-innovation-scoreboard_en. [21]

Goos, M., A. Manning and A. Salomons (2014), "Explaining job polarization: Routine-biased technological change and offshoring", *American Economic Review*, Vol. 104/8, pp. 2509-2526, https://doi.org/10.1257/aer.104.8.2509. [16]

Grossman, G. and E. Helpman (1990), "Trade, innovation, and growth", *The American Economic Review*, Vol. 80/2, pp. 86-91, http://www.jstor.org/stable/2006548 (accessed on 9 November 2020). [17]

Lengyel, B. et al. (2020), "The role of geography in the complex diffusion of innovations", *Scientific Reports*, Vol. 10/1, https://doi.org/10.1038/s41598-020-72137-w. [24]

Maloney, W. and F. Valencia Caicedo (2022), "Engineering growth", *Journal of the European Economic Association*, https://doi.org/10.1093/jeea/jvac014. [27]

McCann, P. (2019), "Perceptions of regional inequality and the geography of discontent: Insights from the UK", *Regional Studies*, Vol. 54/2, pp. 256-267, https://doi.org/10.1080/00343404.2019.1619928. [11]

OECD (2021), *Policies for Present and Future Service Delivery Across Territories*, OECD, Paris. [2]

OECD (2020), *Rural Well-being: Geography of Opportunities*, OECD Rural Studies, OECD Publishing, Paris, https://doi.org/10.1787/d25cef80-en. [1]

OECD (2019), *OECD Regional Outlook 2019: Leveraging Megatrends for Cities and Rural Areas*, OECD Publishing, Paris, https://doi.org/10.1787/9789264312838-en. [19]

OECD (2016), *OECD Regional Outlook 2016: Productive Regions for Inclusive Societies*, OECD Publishing, Paris, https://doi.org/10.1787/9789264260245-en. [3]

OECD (2014), *Innovation and Modernising the Rural Economy*, OECD Rural Policy Reviews, OECD Publishing, Paris, https://doi.org/10.1787/9789264205390-en. [18]

OECD (2013), *Regions and Innovation: Collaborating across Borders*, OECD Reviews of Regional Innovation, OECD Publishing, Paris, https://doi.org/10.1787/9789264205307-en. [22]

OECD (forthcoming), *Innovation Diffusion Across Regions*, OECD, Paris. [6]

Pekkala Kerr, S. and W. Kerr (2020), "Immigrant entrepreneurship in America: Evidence from the survey of business owners 2007 & 2012", *Research Policy*, Vol. 49/3, p. 103918, https://doi.org/10.1016/j.respol.2019.103918. [4]

Romer, P. (1990), "Endogenous technological change", *Journal of Political Economy*, Vol. 98/5 (part 2), pp. S71-S102, https://www.jstor.org/stable/2937632. [8]

Solow, R. (1957), "Technical change and the aggregate production function", *The Review of Economics and Statistics*, pp. 312-320. [12]

Sorenson, O. (2018), "Innovation policy in a networked world", *Innovation Policy and the Economy*, Vol. 18, pp. 53-77, https://doi.org/10.1086/694407. [25]

Notes

[1] This refers to, for example, shifts in age structure of economies and ageing of societies, among other traits.

[2] This includes management and marketing practices.

3 Innovation measurement through a rural lens

How we define innovation in rural regions has an impact on how policies are designed. This chapter examines indicators that are relevant for unlocking innovation in rural regions. It first describes definitions on rural regions that are internationally comparable. Then is summarises measures of innovation most relevant for rural regions.

Understanding innovation in rural regions starts with first defining what is considered rural and what is meant by innovation. Building on the Rural Well-being framework (OECD, 2020[11]), the underlying premise of this work is that, on average, innovation occurs and affects societies differently in rural regions than in urban regions. This may be due to the underlying sectoral, occupational and territorial attributes that characterise low-density areas with longer distances from metropolitan functional urban areas (FUAs). Critically, to the furthest extent possible, the OECD considers a continuum of territories rather than the traditional dichotomy of urban and rural.

Defining rural using physical and driving distances within administrative boundaries

Rural is everywhere and exists as a continuum. What we commonly understand as rural is implicitly spatial and relative. In practice, governments delineate typologies of territories but there is no clear cut-off between regions or areas. Rural characteristics can exist within more urbanised regions and rural attributes are apparent across the spectrum of territorial characteristics. This continuum of rurality is delineated in the recent OECD publication on rural well-being (OECD, 2020[11]).

The term rural is often used to describe territories that have relatively low-density human settlement patterns, with relatively large distances to more densely populated areas. Often, rural regions are characterised as regions with activities closely related to natural resource industries such as mining and agriculture. However, this sectoral definition overlooks many of the different varieties of rural territories and what this means for political agenda-setting in rural regions. Indeed, a region that is identified as "rural" has implications on government finance and wider regional policy making.

In consultation with OECD national governments, the OECD harmonised a set of guidelines for classifying territorial characteristics across countries that avoid the traditional, and sometimes harmful, rural-urban dichotomy. This unified definition of rural[1] provides the basis for analysis across countries within rural economies (OECD, 2020[11]). The most recent definitions of rural regions have benefitted from a reflection on the combination of physical ("first-nature") and human ("second-nature") geographies. Rural regions are defined by economic remoteness, with three distinct features related to the *physical distance to major markets*, *economic connectedness* and *sector specialisation.* Considering these features, rural regions are physically distant from major markets, with specialisation in niche markets and those linked with natural resources such as agriculture and tourism. The degree of economic connectedness with surrounding areas may vary by relative density, infrastructure availability and complementarities between and within rural or urban regions.

The degree of economic and physical connectedness and access to natural resources has an impact on how and what firms and individuals innovate. As such, in accessible rural regions, firms and individuals are more likely to innovate to meet the needs of local and accessible markets, with easier access to both supply chains, regional commercial markets and relative advantages sometimes related to the costs of living and relatively easier access to basic services. This includes, for example, firms in the manufacturing or services sector. In more remote regions, firms and individuals may have a relative comparative advantage in innovating in the agricultural or services sectors. However, because these are areas that often suffer from more limited access to markets and basic government services, innovation and productivity activities take place to first overcome these barriers and then bring new products and processes to the market or firm.

At a geographical scale, we use a variety of definitions to discuss innovation as it concerns rural areas: Territorial Level 2 (TL2)[2] and the share of non-metropolitan populations within each TL2 region at the largest scale; the degree of urbanisation, which is based on grid-level classification at lower scales; and Territorial Level 3 (TL3) at an intermediate level (for further description, please see Box 3.1). The preferred level of territorial analysis in this report will be the most recent adopted definitions of territorial disaggregation elaborated recently by Fadic et al. (2019[2]) in Box 3.1, based on TL3. When there are limitations in the availability of analytical tools, alternative measures are also used. The order of priority for rural definitions in this report is the following:

- **Territorial typology based on access to cities** by Fadic et al. (2019[2]). This is feasible if the analysis is available at least at TL3 or lower, which roughly corresponds to the third highest level of territorial classifications in most OECD countries. In previous years, some of the analysis is only available in older classification systems that identify TL3 regions as predominantly urban, intermediate and predominantly rural regions.
- **The degree of urbanisation** identifies rural areas, towns and suburbs, and cities separately. Data are assessed at the grid level.
- **The degree of rurality** based on the share of populations within TL2 that are living outside FUA (non-metro) regions. This allows for data to be analysed on the TL2 regions with an indicator of relative shares of rural populations based on OECD internal estimates of TL3 regions.

To the furthest extent possible, national rural comparisons will not be used for rural analysis.

Box 3.1. Classifications of rural regions

In 2019, the OECD published a new classification that is based on functional urban areas (FUAs) that incorporates density and the driving estimations for the time it takes to access dense metropolitan areas. To the furthest extent possible, rural will be defined as one of three types of small regions (TL3) with less than 50% of the regional population living in metropolitan areas. This includes rural regions inside FUAs (where at least 50% of the population lives within a 1-hour driving distance away from a dense urban area with a population larger than 250 000 inhabitants), rural regions close to small or medium cities of populations smaller or equivalent to 250 000 inhabitants, and rural remote areas. When this is not possible, the second-best definition will include the degree of urbanisation classification that consists of cities, towns and suburbs, and rural areas. The degree of urbanisation is applied to a global estimated population grid for the years 1975, 1990, 2000 and 2015 and projections up to 2050 (see Annex 1.D). This allows the report to show the trends in urbanisation over 75 years with unprecedented international comparability. The degree of urbanisation was designed to create a simple and neutral method that could be applied in every country in the world. It relies primarily on population size and density thresholds applied to a population grid with cells of 1 by 1 km. Roughly speaking:

1. Cities consist of contiguous grid cells that have a density of at least 1 500 inhabitants per km^2 or are at least 50% built up. They must have a population of at least 50 000 inhabitants.
2. Towns and semi-dense areas consist of contiguous grid cells with a density of at least 300 inhabitants per km^2 and are at least 3% built up. They must have a total population of at least 5 000 inhabitants.
3. Rural areas are cells that do not belong to a city or a town and are semi-dense areas. Most of these have a density below 300 inhabitants per km^2.

Finally, when no other method of measurement is available, we will use the degree of rurality within large regions (TL2) or the country. This is based on a simple calculation of the population total within each of the five access to city typologies over the total TL2 or country population. We then take the three non-metropolitan categories within the Access to City typology in the entire population as a proxy for the degree of rurality of the TL2 region or country.

The diverse types of rural regions all have different characteristics and policy needs. There are three types of non-metropolitan regions that are considered, to various degrees, to share rural more rural characteristics than urban ones. Non-metropolitan regions (NMRs) are defined as having less than

50% of the population living in an FUA with a population larger than 250 000 inhabitants. The three types of NMRs include regions with access to a metropolitan region, non-metropolitan areas with access to a small- or medium-sized city, and non-metropolitan regions in remote areas.

- **Non-metropolitan regions with access to a metropolitan region:** These regions have 50% or more of the regional population that lives within a 60-minute drive to a metropolitan area. This is similar in part to towns and suburbs surrounding the distant periphery of major metropolitan centres. An example of such regions includes Tyrolean Oberland in Austria (AT334), Montmagny in Quebec, Canada (CA2418), Jura in France (FRC22) and Nagasaki in Japan (JPJ42). The challenges of such regions are often tied to economies of metropolitan areas, while focusing on industries such as tourism, without some of the infrastructure barriers of less densely populated areas.

- **Non-metropolitan regions with access to small- or medium-sized cities:** These are regions with 50% or more of the regional population living within a 60-minute drive from a small- or medium-sized city. Examples of these types of regions include the administrative district of Neufchâteau in Belgium (BE344), San Antonio in Chile (CL056), South Bohemia in the Czech Republic (CZ031), East Lancashire in the United Kingdom (UKD46) and Springfield in Illinois, United States (US158). These regions have a strong manufacturing base and linkages to neighbouring economies.

- **Non-metropolitan regions without access to cities (remote):** These are regions with 50% or more of the regional population without access to an FUA (metropolitan) within a 60-minute drive. Examples of such areas include West Estonia in Estonia (EE004), Lapland in Finland (FI1D7), Sonneberg in Germany (DEG0H) and Lesbos in Greece (EL411). Rural remote areas have economies with fewer interlinkages with major cities and often focus on tourism, while rural remote regions, such as those in Canada, Chile, Colombia, Finland, Mexico and the United States (US) often also have an important share of the population with an Indigenous heritage that face distinct challenges.

The schematic breakdown is available in the figure below.

Figure 3.1. OECD typology for access to cities

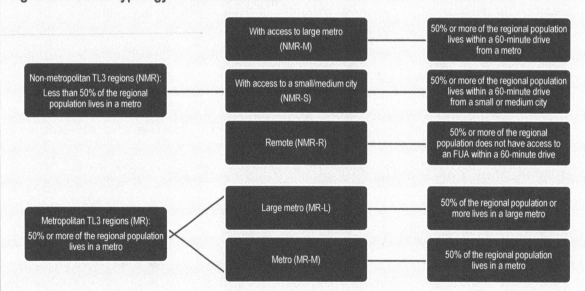

Note: Large metro: an FUA with a population larger than 1.5 million inhabitants; Metro: an FUA with a population larger than 250 000 inhabitants; Small or medium city: an FUA with a population smaller or equal to 250 000 inhabitants.
Source: Fadic, M. et al. (2019[2]) (2019), "Classifying small (TL3) regions based on metropolitan population, low density and remoteness", https://dx.doi.org/10.1787/b902cc00-en.

A fresh look at measuring innovation in rural regions

Innovation, according to the 4th revision of the Oslo Manual, is defined as "a new or improved product or process (or combination thereof) that differs significantly from the unit's previous products or processes and that has been made available to potential users (product) or brought into use by the unit (process)" (OECD/Eurostat, 2018[3]). The recent revision of the manual now includes definitions specifically for the business sector that targets product and process innovations, including management practices, that have previously not been introduced to the market or brought to use by the firm as well as innovation-related activities that include developmental, financial and commercial activities intending to result in an innovation.

Box 3.2. Defining Innovation from the 4th revision of the Oslo Manual, 2018

What is the Oslo Manual?

The Oslo Manual is a publication that outlines a commonly agreed upon approach to measure and report statistics on innovations. Starting in the early 1990s, the Oslo Manual was elaborated through the consensus of the OECD Working Party of National Experts on Science and Technology Indicators (NESTI) and has been adopted by over 80 countries. The guidance outlined in the manual is used by major international organisations and researchers worldwide. Its revision was conducted through consultation with both the NESTI and Eurostat's Community Innovation Survey (CIS) Taskforce.

Defining innovation

The 4th edition of the Oslo Manual distinguishes between innovation as an outcome (an innovation) and the activities by which innovations come about (innovation activities). It defines an innovation as "a new or improved product or process (or combination thereof) that differs significantly from the unit's previous products or processes and that has been made available to potential users (product) or brought into use by the unit (process)" (OECD/Eurostat, 2018[3]).

The major additions to the previous versions include: measuring innovation not only from businesses but also from other organisations and individuals; updates to improve harmonisation between core definitions and taxation; better accounting of globalisation, digitalisation and trends in investment in intangible assets; guidance on measuring internal and external factors influencing business innovation; prioritisation of the measurements of government policies on innovation; expansion on methodological guidelines; guidance on the use of innovation data and a new glossary.

Source: OECD (n.d.[4]), Oslo Manual 2018, https://www.oecd.org/sti/inno/oslo-manual-2018-info.pdf; OECD/Eurostat (2018[3]), *Oslo Manual 2018: Guidelines for Collecting, Reporting and Using Data on Innovation, 4th Edition*, https://dx.doi.org/10.1787/9789264304604-en.

The original definition is broad and encompasses, without particular prejudice, all product and process innovation, which includes difficult-to-categorise innovations such as innovation in business models and social innovation. However, most indicators that are not based on surveys focus on measurable outcomes of activities regularly associated with innovation in high-technology (high-tech) and high-value industries. Unfortunately, many governments also specifically focus innovation strategies on high-tech industries, leaving innovation in all other industries and activities without the same level of support. Indicators based on surveys have the capacity to track incremental innovations and innovations that may be more standard in non-technical industries. Yet, for rural innovation, the challenge is often that surveys rarely have a large enough sample size to truly measure trends in rural areas.

The analysis in this report departs from traditional science and technology innovation measurement tools to prioritise measurement methods best suited to understanding innovation regions with rural characteristics. While encouraging innovation is a priority for many governments, gathering and analysing data on innovation specifically in rural regions is a challenge due to measurement, representativeness (survey sample size) and confidentiality concerns.

Innovation can be measured using a variety of tools, each with advantages and disadvantages for rural areas. The following types of measures are elaborated below and summarised in Table 3.1.

- **Self-reported measures of innovation** are often a useful method for understanding firm processes and outputs. While innovation surveys often directly ask for output related to innovations in the production of new goods and services, in practice, it is often easier for governments and researchers to capture *product* rather than *process* innovation and often difficult to agree on what is "new" about innovation using innovation surveys (Hall, 2011[5]). In addition to this bias, innovation surveys often suffer from limited coverage and lack of territorial representativeness in rural areas.

- **Product-level data** (for example, production or export statistics) has the potential to capture new-to-market and new-to-firm innovation in products, through innovation surveys, or through balance sheets or export product-level data. This type of data can still capture "new to firm" product innovations (vertical differentiation) and "new to market products" or diversification (horizontal differentiation) (Braguinsky et al., 2020[6]). However, accessing these sources of data is notoriously difficult on a territorially disaggregate level that allows analysis more accurately identify areas with rural attributes and are often more relevant for the manufacturing sector.

- Another popular innovation measure is **research and development (R&D) investment or jobs**. This type of measure has its advantages as it measures innovation in comparative units (currency or number of workers) but it cannot measure success or quality of input (investments and workers). In the case of start-ups receiving venture capital, R&D investment can also be considered an indicator of a low innovative capacity per input (OECD, 2020[7]). There is also apparent randomness to the outputs associated with R&D investments and jobs, as the payoffs of some types of human and capital investment take a longer time to come to fruition. Furthermore, due to headquarters bias, in most cases, R&D investment and jobs are often reported at the level of the headquarter of the firm, rather than the plant location, which leads to a systematic and territorial underestimation in rural regions. Between the two forms of indicators, R&D jobs, and in particular the share of R&D jobs within firms, is the preferred measure of the relative importance of innovation within firms.

- In the 1980s, researchers began exploring the use of **patents** as a measure of innovation success (Pakes and Griliches, 1980[8]).[3] Half a century later, patents remain one of the most commonly used measures of innovation, but are heavily critiqued for sectoral, size and territorial biases and can also be associated with anticompetitive behaviour.[4] For rural areas, patents are valuable measures if they are adjusted for relevant occupations, even if they only capture a segment of local economies.

- One of the oldest proxies for innovation is looking at firm-level outcomes such as **high growth** or **productivity** and its residual value. The measure is capable of measuring outcomes in a comparable manner but it is not clear whether growth and productivity are specifically the outcome of innovation, or changes in markets outside of the decision-making process of the firm. This measure also often suffers from headquarter bias.[5]

- **Start-up entrepreneurship** can be used as a proxy for firms that are likely to adopt new ways of producing goods and services. While no direct measure is taken of whether or not new methods and practices are adopted, new entrants have more incentives to use updated methods and tools with leaner business models and less institutional clutter. However, without production data or business surveys, it is also difficult to directly understand whether start-ups are productive and scalable, or if they are rather placeholders, fiscal havens, "zombie firms" or simply self-employed persons on precarious contracts. In rural areas, however, focusing on start-up activities avoids at least some of the sectoral and compositional issues with other measures of innovation.

Table 3.1. Common innovation measures and relevance to rural regions

Measurement method	Advantages	Disadvantages	Suitable for rural regions	Examples
Innovation surveys	Direct measurement of activities within firms	• Subjectivity bias Headquarter bias	• Yes, if can avoid small sample bias in subnational levels	• European Union (EU) Community Innovation Survey
Production-level firm data	Measures new firm and market innovations	• Difficult access • More easily available for exporters • Bias in service innovation • Headquarter bias	• Limited suitability better for the manufacturing sector • Limited availability of territorial indicators • Data is often clustered by port of export	• United Nations Conference on Trade and Development-World Bank World Integrated Trade Solution (WITS) • Centre d'études prospectives et d'informations internationales (CEPII) • Atlas of Economic Complexity
R&D jobs or investment	Comparability of measures	• Expected payoffs vary • More relevant for technology and science sectors • More relevant for large firms • Headquarter bias	• Limited suitability • Rural firms are often not as large as firms in more dense areas	• OECD Regional R&D Statistics
Patents	A measure of successful innovations	• Biased towards firms that work in technology and science sectors • May also measure anticompetitive behaviour • Headquarter bias	• Yes, if able to adjust to account for the composition of firms that are likely to patent and territorial endowments	• OECD Regional Patent Indicators
Productivity or high-growth firms	Measures expected outcomes	• Cannot disentangle whether productivity or growth occurred to changes within a firm or further advantages market behaviour • Headquarter bias	• Yes, but may measure innovation absorption capacity better than innovation, and suffers from headquarter bias	• OECD Regional Productivity Indicators
Start-up activities	New entry is more likely to adopt more innovative and new approaches	• Unless you know about production and scale-up, it is difficult to disentangle innovative from non-innovative entrepreneurship	• Yes, but needs to be nuanced	• OECD Regional Database • National resources

Note: Measurement methods reported are the most commonly used measures. There may be others available that have not been discussed.

There are biases in all forms of measurement tools: innovation is not precluded from this bias. All forms of innovation measurements have positive and negative attributes. For clarity and evidence-based policy making, it is important to present the reasoning behind why some measurements of innovation are relatively less suitable for rural areas. The caveats in the suitability of each of the proposed measurement methods for use in the rural context as compared to more urbanised regions can be summarised as biases due to the following:

- **Composition bias**: Bias due to the structure or composition of the economy, including the size and sector of rural firms and the occupational structure of rural labour supply. For example, patents and R&D credits are more often filed in larger firms and those in the manufacturing sector than in smaller firms and most firms in the services and agricultural sectors. Small- and medium-sized enterprises (SMEs) are more likely to participate in incremental innovation.

- **Territorial endowment**: Bias due to pre-existing conditions and opportunities in rural regions that are different from those in denser regions.

- **Headquarter bias**: Bias due to the statistical method of gathering information that often centralises responses from multiple branches to firm headquarters. In most business statistics, data are collected on the enterprise level, associated with the location where business activities are officially declared (headquarters). Often this results in a downward bias for reported activities that is in fact occurring more frequently in less dense areas. Likewise, this includes the location of patents that are often filed at headquarters.

Because of these challenges, several of the regular science- and technology-based indicators are not well-equipped to adequately understand innovation in rural regions.

The composition bias refers to the structure of local economies based on the different characteristics of firms present in rural regions as compared to denser areas. For example, these are related to firm size, sectors and occupation characteristics within territories. Rural regions tend to have smaller firms in less diversified sectors than denser regions. On the contrary, denser areas tend to have larger firms. These larger firms in dense areas are more likely to have easier access to R&D investment, financial and human capital, including legal services, to uphold intellectual property rights. Because the economy of rural regions is composed of smaller firms, they are often less capital-intensive and have more limited access to legal resources, and by default do not demonstrate innovation in the same ways. In rural regions, innovation comes in other forms and has less of a focus on standard product innovations and a comparative advantage in the development of original or incremental innovations more adequately captured in surveys (OECD, 2020[9]; Freshwater et al., 2019[10]; Lee and Rodriguez-Pose, 2012[11]) or those identified as local and community-driven innovation that is a part of what is considered "social innovation" (Jungsberg et al., 2020[12]; Mahroum et al., 2007[13]; Markey, Ryser and Halseth, 2020[14]; Wojan and Parker, 2017[15]).

In a related manner, there are pre-existing territorial endowments that determine the access to land, accessibility to capital stock, transport costs and labour resources in spatial economics (Fitjar and Rodríguez-Pose, 2013[16]; Maloney and Valencia Caicedo, 2022[17]; McCann, 2013[18]) . The difference in endowments (for example, digital and physical infrastructure, natural resources, demographics and access to higher education) in rural versus urban areas would also suggest a downward implicit bias when using R&D and patents as a proxy for innovation. For example, if high-speed Internet connections are needed to develop digital service innovations, then evaluating the innovation capacity of rural regions as compared to denser regions with less access to high-speed connections only informs rural policy makers that more digital infrastructure is needed and not that there is an intrinsic lack of innovative potential.

Finally, headquarter bias is a bias associated with the way in which statistical agencies collect data (Bils, Klenow and Ruane, 2020[19]; OECD, 2017[20]). For some innovation measurement methods, attributing innovation proxies to headquarters is logical; however, the prioritisation of analysis at the headquarters level systematically leaves behind rural areas. For example, investment in R&D often requires capital investments that are shared among different branches of the same firm. The product of R&D investment should benefit outcomes for all branches of the firm (or inversely serve as a mechanism to remove non-productive branches from the structure of the firm).[6] With no headquarter bias, there should be no reason why employment as measured by labour surveys, and employment as measured by firms would be different. However, in many cases, the most commonly used databases do indeed suffer from this bias (OECD, 2017, pp. 27-28[20]).

There is a small but growing economic geography and innovation literature that prioritises the differences between regions as important for understanding and supporting the proliferation of innovation preconditions, processes and outcomes (Crescenzi, 2005[21]; Eder, 2018[22]). In some cases, the differences in the composition and territorial endowments of the region are quite evident. For example, Karlsson and Olsson (1998[23]) argue that large firms tend to need to rely heavily on resources in dense areas to grow, while SMEs can survive more easily in peripheral areas. Likewise, Caragliu, de Dominicus and de Groot (2015[24]) advise focusing on policies that encourage specialisation for low-density regions and diversification of activities in denser areas. In other cases, the difference is due to lower opportunities for local knowledge spill-over and adaption to a more collaborative model (Grillitsch and Nilsson, 2015[25]).

In sum, if the compositional structure and territorial endowments of rural regions mimicked those of denser economies proportionately, then there would be limited reasons why the use of statistics, whether or not they are biased towards manufacturing and science- and technology-intensive sectors, would be different in rural regions. In the sections below, the analysis will provide examples of why this is not currently the case for rural regions today.[7]

A few takeaways from this analysis have impacted the strategy of the report and can be summarised as follows:

- The selection of measurement tools for innovation in rural areas is more often associated with bias, either due to the composition or endowment-related differences across territories.
- Self-reported innovation measures are useful measures of rural innovation but, in practice, they often suffer from insufficient observations on a territorial level.
- Taking into account the structure of rural economies would require adjusting commonly used measures such as R&D and patents to account for the types of innovation that are more common in rural regions.
- Focusing on innovation proxies such as entrepreneurship and start-up activities may be better suited for understanding drivers of innovation in rural areas, as it both avoids headquarter bias and its measurement is not likely to be directly affected by the compositional characteristics of rural areas.

Better indicators can give us a more accurate picture of innovation in rural areas

Standard measures of innovation such as patents and R&D statistics are often better at measuring innovation in highly concentrated, urbanised areas. Innovation, as measured by patents, can vary substantially between countries and regions. For example, in Figure 3.2, patent applications per million inhabitants are highly dispersed across TL2 regions. Regions with the highest level of patents per application are often regions with major large metropolitan cities, with strong links with research universities, strong information technology (IT) sectors or a strong manufacturing sector. On the right side of the second panel, the regions with the highest level of patents per million inhabitants are in Bavaria (DE2) containing the manufacturing capital Munich in Germany, the capital region of Korea (KR01), California, US (US06) consisting of Silicon Valley[8], and Southern-Kanto, Japan (JPD) containing the capital Tokyo.

Figure 3.2. Patents in regions (TL2), patent applications, 2019

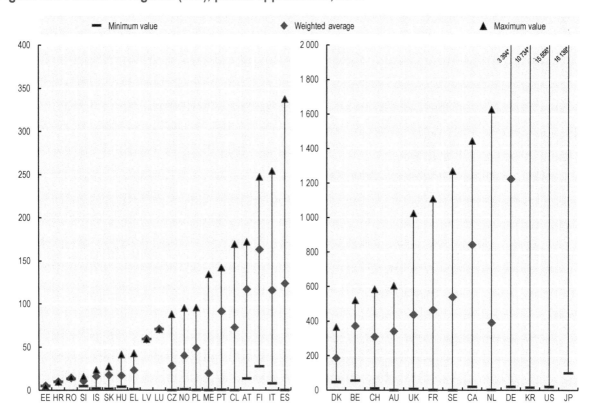

Note: Graphs include regional (TL2) data on OECD countries with available data. In some countries, multiple regions have zero patent applications. The data are presented separately on two graphs because of the readability of different scales. The graph on the left only presents countries with up to 350 applicants in 2019, while the graph on the right represents those with over 350 and above.
* Maximum value.
Source: OECD calculations based on European Patent Office (2019[26]), *European Patent Register*, https://www.epo.org/searching-for-patents/business/patstat.html.

However, patents, as a proxy for innovation, lack the capacity to account for the occupational and sectoral structure of rural regions. In the example above, the major regions with patents are either capital regions that have easier access to finance and auxiliary services, or regions with university interlinkages focusing on IT, medical and science-based work and, in the case of Germany, a strong manufacturing sector. This regional finding is also in line with national trends in sectors that are self-reported as innovative.

Adjusting for the occupational structure of economies improves the perception of innovation in rural regions. The general lack of innovation activity as measured through patenting could be in part due to the lack of relevant labour supply. Following the recent work by Dotzel (2017[27]) and Wojan (2021[28]) who generated classifications for occupations that showed a higher likelihood of patenting,[9] we adjust the number of patents to the occupations where professionals are more likely to patent (Annex Table 3.D.1).

On a regional (TL2) level, taking this additional step demonstrates the sensitivity of patent intensity (patent to population ratio) statistics to the structure of the economy (Annex Figure 3.D.2). However, the regional (TL2) level only shows part of the picture. While descriptive, the regional (TL2) level demonstrates that the degree to which patent intensity relates to the share of rural in each TL2 is increasingly negative when patent intensity is adjusted by occupation. In both adjusted and non-adjusted cases, the relationship is not statistically different from zero. This is likely due to the fact that the regional (TL2) level may be too aggregate to determine if the adjustment can make a difference.[10] Further diving into the level of smaller regions (TL3), evidence from the US demonstrates that the picture for rural regions changes (Figures 3.3 and 3.4).

Patenting intensity is strongly associated with the occupational choices of individuals. The greater the number of individuals with occupations that participate in registered inventions in a small TL3 region, the more likely the region will have registered inventions. The territorial share of occupations involving inventive activities does a better job at targetting geographical disparity of innovation capacity than patent applicants alone. In Figure 3.3, the map of the US is filled with the average yearly number of patents (Panel A) and the average yearly number of patents per occupation where individuals have incentives to register patents (Panel B). Both maps demonstrate that there is some clustering of activities. However, the differences in the density of this measure of innovation diffuses across space as we move from the initial pure patent-based measures to adjusted measures that account for the territorial distribution of occupations where patents are commonplace.

Figure 3.3. Patents and inventive occupations in the US

A. Yearly average of patents filed on a county level, 2000-15

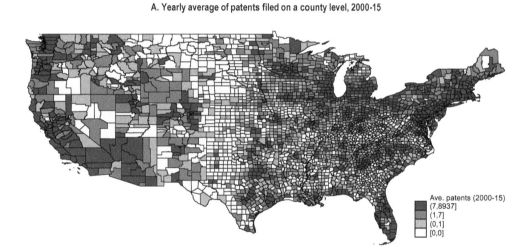

B. Yearly average of patents filed per inventive occupation on a county level

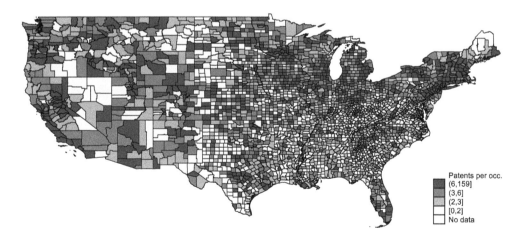

Note: Inventive occupations as defined by Dotzel and Wojan (2021[28]).
Source: Wojan, T. (2021[28]), "An occupational approach for analyzing regional invention", https://ncses.nsf.gov/pubs/ncses22202/assets/ncses22202.pdf.

Figure 3.4. Patents and inventive occupations in the US, by typology

Patents filed, 2015, versus the ratio of patents filed per 1 000 individuals with inventive occupations

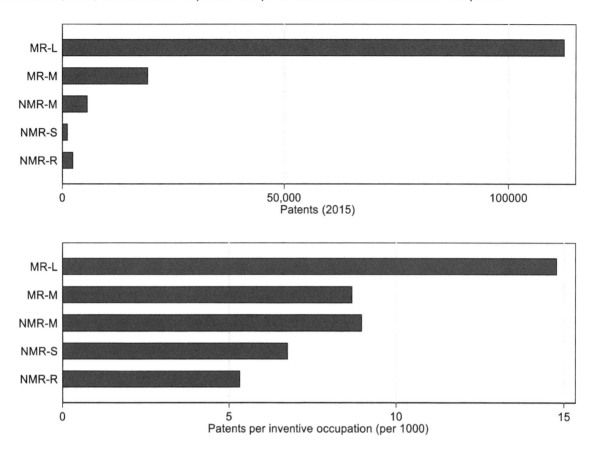

Note: Inventive occupations as defined by Dotzel and Wojan (2021[28]). MR-L refers to large metropolitan regions that have 50% or more of the population that lives in an FUA with 1.5 million inhabitants or more; MR-M refers to metropolitan regions with a population of 250 000 inhabitants and where 50% or more of the regional population lives in an FUA; NMR-M refers to non-metropolitan regions with access to an FUA within a 60-minute drive and less than 250 000 inhabitants; NMR-S refers to regions where 50% or more of the regional population lives within 1-hour access to a small- or medium-sized city; NMR-R refers to a non-metropolitan region where 50% or more of the regional population does not have access to an FUA within a 60-minute drive. Patents filed in 2015 were 112 379 (MR-L), 19 264 (MR-M), 5 670 (NMR-M), 1 220 (NMR-S) and 2 427 (NMR-R). The patents per inventive occupation (per 1 000 individuals) rates are the following: 14.8 (MR-L), 8.7 (MR-M), 9.0 (NMR-M), 6.7 (NMR-S) and 5.3 (NMR-R). The typology is based on aggregating data from the county level.
Source: Dotzel, K. and T. Wojan (2021[28]), "An occupational approach for analyzing regional invention", https://ncses.nsf.gov/pubs/ncses2220 2/assets/ncses22202.pdf.

There is a 16-fold decrease in the disparity between non-metropolitan regions and metropolitan regions when adjusting the patent intensity to account for occupational distributions. Grouping metropolitan and non-metropolitan classifications together, regions in large and medium metropolitan regions (MR-L and MR-M) in the US have approximately 13 times more patents than non-metropolitan regions (NMR-M, NMR-S and NMR-R in Figure 3.4). When we adjust for the occupations prominent in territories, the disparity falls starkly to close to 0.8.

Out of 1 000 individuals with inventive occupations in non-metropolitan regions close to cities, 9 individuals filed for patents, in 2015. In comparison, in medium-sized metropolitan regions, 8.7 patents were filed. However, a gap remains between individuals in non-metropolitan regions and large metropolitan areas. Inventive individuals in non-metropolitan regions on average produced six less patents than those in large metropolitan regions.

This simple accounting practice demonstrates how the structure of rural economies is important when determining how to measure innovation. Rural regions have different resources and opportunities and are by definition different from more dense areas where there are higher shares of occupations with inventors who are more likely to patent. Firms in rural regions tend to more often be small, in some cases, older, and have a close connection to natural resources, either in agriculture or those based on natural resources (mining, agri-tourism, etc). In understanding rural innovation, patent ratios should be adjusted for the structure of the rural economy.

Rural regions are structured differently, both in occupations and sectors. Occupations in which applying for patents is commonplace are not evenly distributed across territories. In the US, the inventive class (occupations in sectors with a high association with inventions) is clustered on the coasts and in the northeastern region (Figure 3.3).[11] There is a much higher share of inventive jobs per inhabitant in metropolitan areas as compared to non-metropolitan regions with various levels of access to urbanised cities.

In Canada and the US, most individuals in occupations that participate in the process of applying for patents are located in larger metropolitan regions (Figure 3.5 in Canada and Annex Figure 3.D.1 in the US). In metropolitan areas of the US, for every 1 000 individuals in the active labour force, there are close to 20 more who have occupations in which patents are more common practice, as compared to non-metropolitan regions. For those who have such occupations, the act of patenting (or trademarking) can be as a result of claiming intellectual property rights over pure or incremental innovations or alternatively be due to anticompetitive behaviour or as part of a human resource key performance indicator practice within firms.

Figure 3.5. Inventive occupations in Canada, 2019

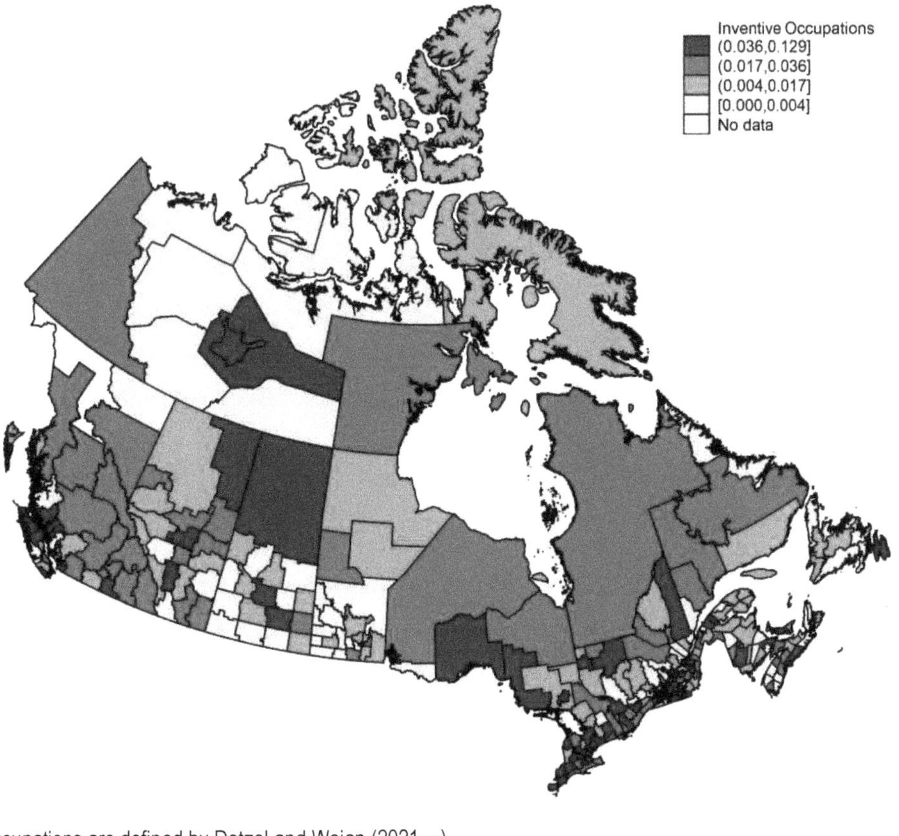

Note: Inventive occupations are defined by Dotzel and Wojan (2021[28]).
Source: OECD calculations based on Statistics Canada (2016[29]), *Census of Population*, Statistics Canada Catalogue no. 98-400-X2016295.

The implications of an unequal distribution of occupations across territories are important for innovation policies. Focusing on policies to increase innovation that are frequently associated with patents (i.e. R&D subsidies or tax breaks) in regions where there are few to no individuals in such occupations, is misguided. It is equally misguided to consider that areas with no or very few patents are not innovative because there are no patents in the region.

A viable solution is to focus on encouraging the framework conditions to enhance the innovation processes and activities that are more common in rural areas. Whenever possible, focusing on relevant indicators of innovation in rural areas and on framework conditions or entrepreneurship should be prioritised. If this is not possible, it is important that traditional indicators account for the intensity of such activities relative to the appropriate shares of sectors or occupations. Individuals in rural regions have a comparative advantage in entrepreneurship and different forms of innovation are more common in the periphery (Rodríguez-Pose and Fitjar, 2013[30]; Mayer, 2020[31]; Shearmur and Doloreux, 2016[32]).[12]

A few important takeaways can be understood from this territorial analysis on innovation indicators.

- **Traditional stories on patents do not give a precise image of innovation in rural regions**. Rural regions are simply structured differently than dense regions: therefore, how we measure innovation matters. Governments and researchers need to use relevant statistics for comparing innovation measures and population parameters.
- **Individuals' occupations are important drivers of innovation**. The types of activities people do matter. Encouraging the retention or attractiveness of individuals with occupations where invention is more frequent can spur innovation-driven growth in rural regions.
  - For rural innovation, policy makers should focus on encouraging innovation in activities that have more opportunities to **adapt to the comparative advantages of rural regions**.

Beyond the national science and technology framework for innovation in rural regions

When we are looking to understand and promote rural innovation, **the way we measure innovation matters**. Conventional definitions and measures are often better suited for product (rather than process) innovation occurring in large firms. Definitions and measures of innovative activities are often a better match for innovations in large firms that engage in product rather than process innovation, are focused on the manufacturing or R&D intensive sectors and depend on heavier capital and resource expenditures. However, a larger share of firms in rural regions are often small and focused on the service or natural resource sectors (Freshwater et al., 2019[10]) where innovation is incremental or is characterised by strong use of social and human capital (Shearmur, Carrincazeaux and Doloreux, 2016[33]; Simonen and McCann, 2008[34]; 2010[35]).

Continuing to overlook the geography of innovation is a missed opportunity, has exacerbated pre-existing territorial divides and overlooks some of the prime opportunities for growth. In addition to the findings of this report, forthcoming analysis from field studies also finds important evidence to continue to reinforce the importance of integrating geography into innovation studies.

- From Switzerland, using territorial indicators demonstrates that investment in traditional innovation activities such as R&D are associated with more jobs and inward expenditures in rural regions, while this is not the case in metropolitan areas. For example, in 2019, close to 35 cents per Swiss franc spent on R&D was outsourced; in rural regions, only 4 cents per Swiss franc left the firm for R&D expenses (OECD, forthcoming[36]).

- Using innovation surveys for measuring innovation in Scotland shows that while geography impacts the structure of the economy, innovators are inherently the same across regions. The age (young) and size (large) of firms are important in determining whether they innovate or not. Furthermore, national innovation and productivity can be increased by focusing on rural regions that still have strong opportunities to grow and where the return to innovation is still relatively large (OECD, forthcoming[37]).

Lastly, policy makers and academics focus on rents and networks to understand innovation clusters and locational choices for firms, but *people* clustering is also critical since individuals are the true drivers of innovation, as demonstrated earlier with patent statistics in Canada and the US and several academic studies (Florida, 2002[38]; McCann and Arita, 2006[39]; Van Oort, 2017[40]). The pre-existing focus on national science, technology and innovation (STI) measures is partially due to data limitations and the difficulty involved in measuring innovation, but sometimes can also be explained by a lack of contextual prioritisation.

In light of this, the structure of the analysis in this report prioritises a territorial, individual capacity-based approach to innovation (creation and adoption) on three different levels, as outlined in Figure 3.6. This report suggests a new framework that overcomes some of the biases outlined above. It moreover focuses on measurement and policies to improve the capacity to innovate, by looking at the characteristics of entrepreneurs that are more likely to innovate.

Figure 3.6. Analytical framework for understanding the drivers of innovation in rural regions

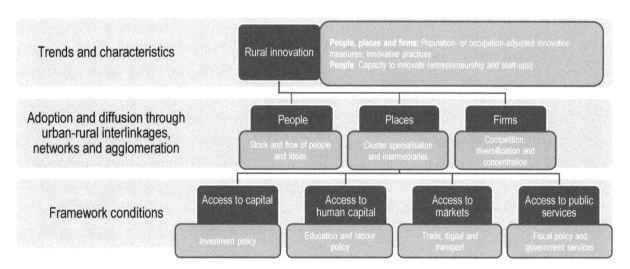

Note: Public services include direct support mechanisms.

As described in the analytical framework and in line with the literature and the relative importance of innovation diffusion and adoption in rural regions, the subsequent publications will also address: the approach to understanding network and agglomeration effects and how they amplify innovation adoption through rural-urban interlinkage mechanisms and include the role of different actors such as academia, industry and the public sector; and the framework conditions that are vital to the proliferation of the creation of new products and processes as well as the diffusion of innovation across territories, including through advanced business services specifically targeted at innovation and SMEs.

In sum, there are two main takeaways from this analysis. First, common perceptions of rural areas with low innovation merit further contextual reflection. Second, precisely measuring innovation in rural areas is a challenge. Second-best measurement methods should be nuanced to capture structural and resource endowments in rural regions. When possible, using survey-based innovation measures with a large enough sample of observation from firms and individuals in rural regions should be prioritised. When this is not available, adjusting indicators to reflect the relevant sectoral, size and occupation structure should be reinforced. Lastly, as will be explored further below, individuals' capacity to innovate by looking at drivers of entrepreneurship and new firms should be explored. For many rural regions, supporting young entrepreneurship can be particularly advantageous.

The following chapter explores innovation in rural regions and areas, prioritising a capacity approach to innovation that include factors associated with innovation such as inventors, firm demographics, entrepreneurship and social innovation. It follows with a brief chapter on outcomes closely associated with innovation including high growth and productivity.

References

Bils, M., P. Klenow and C. Ruane (2020), "Misallocation or mismeasurement?", National Bureau of Economic Research, Cambridge, MA, https://doi.org/10.3386/w26711. [19]

Braguinsky, S. et al. (2020), "Product innovation, product diversification, and firm growth: Evidence from Japan's early industrialization", National Bureau of Economic Research, Cambridge, MA, https://doi.org/10.3386/w26665. [6]

Caragliu, A., L. de Dominicis and H. de Groot (2015), "Both Marshall and Jacobs were right!", *Economic Geography*, Vol. 92/1, pp. 87-111, https://doi.org/10.1080/00130095.2015.1094371. [24]

Crescenzi, R. (2005), "Innovation and regional growth in the enlarged Europe: The role of local innovative capabilities, peripherality, and education", *Growth and Change*, Vol. 36/4, pp. 471-507, https://doi.org/10.1111/j.1468-2257.2005.00291.x. [21]

Dotzel, K. (2017), "Three essays on human capital and innovation in the United States", Chapter 3, Graduate School of the Ohio State University. [27]

Dotzel, K. and T. Wojan (2021), "An occupational approach for analyzing regional invention", National Center for Science and Engineering Statistics, https://ncses.nsf.gov/pubs/ncses22202/assets/ncses22202.pdf. [28]

Eder, J. (2018), "Innovation in the periphery: A critical survey and research agenda", *International Regional Science Review*, Vol. 42/2, pp. 119-146, https://doi.org/10.1177/0160017618764279. [22]

European Patent Office (2019), *European Patent Register*, https://www.epo.org/searching-for-patents/business/patstat.html. [26]

Fadic, M. et al. (2019), "Classifying small (TL3) regions based on metropolitan population, low density and remoteness", *OECD Regional Development Working Papers*, No. 2019/06, OECD Publishing, Paris, https://doi.org/10.1787/b902cc00-en. [2]

Fitjar, R. and A. Rodríguez-Pose (2013), "Firm collaboration and modes of innovation in Norway", *Research Policy*, Vol. 42/1, pp. 128-138, https://doi.org/10.1016/j.respol.2012.05.009. [16]

Florida, R. (2002), *The Rise of the Creative Class*, Basic Books, New York. [38]

Freshwater, D. et al. (2019), "Business development and the growth of rural SMEs", *OECD Regional Development Working Papers*, No. 2019/07, OECD Publishing, Paris, https://doi.org/10.1787/74256611-en. [10]

Govindarajan, V. and J. Euchner (2012), "Reverse innovation", *Research-Technology Management*, Vol. 55/6, pp. 13-17, https://doi.org/10.5437/08956308x5506003. [43]

Grillitsch, M. and M. Nilsson (2015), "Innovation in peripheral regions: Do collaborations compensate for a lack of local knowledge spillovers?", *The Annals of Regional Science*, Vol. 54/1, pp. 299-321, https://doi.org/10.1007/s00168-014-0655-8. [25]

Hall, B. (2020), "Patents, innovation, and development", National Bureau of Economic Research, Cambridge, MA, https://doi.org/10.3386/w27203. [42]

Hall, B. (2011), "Innovation and productivity", National Bureau of Economic Research, Cambridge, MA, https://doi.org/10.3386/w17178. [5]

Hall, B., C. Helmers and G. von Graevenitz (2015), "Technology entry in the presence of patent thickets", National Bureau of Economic Research, Cambridge, MA, https://doi.org/10.3386/w21455. [41]

Jungsberg, L. et al. (2020), "Key actors in community-driven social innovation in rural areas in the Nordic countries", *Journal of Rural Studies*, Vol. 79, pp. 276-285, https://doi.org/10.1016/j.jrurstud.2020.08.004. [12]

Karlsson, C. and O. Olsson (1998), "Product innovation in small and large enterprises", *Small Business Economics*, Vol. 10/1, pp. 31-46, https://doi.org/10.1023/a:1007970416484. [23]

Lee, N. and A. Rodriguez-Pose (2012), "Innovation and spatial inequality in Europe and USA", *Journal of Economic Geography*, Vol. 13/1, pp. 1-22, https://doi.org/10.1093/jeg/lbs022. [11]

Mahroum, S. et al. (2007), "Rural innovation". [13]

Maloney, W. and F. Valencia Caicedo (2022), "Engineering growth", *Journal of the European Economic Association*, https://doi.org/10.1093/jeea/jvac014. [17]

Markey, S., L. Ryser and G. Halseth (2020), "The critical role of services during crisis and recovery: Learning from smarter services and infrastructure projects". [14]

Mayer, H. (2020), "Slow Innovation in Europe's Peripheral Regions: Innovation beyond Acceleration", *ISR-Forschungsberichte*, Vol. 51, pp. 8-21, https://doi.org/10.1553/isr_fb051s8. [31]

McCann, P. (2013), *Modern Urban and Regional Economics*, Oxford University Press. [18]

McCann, P. and T. Arita (2006), "Clusters and regional development: Some cautionary observations from the semiconductor industry", *Information Economics and Policy*, Vol. 18/2, pp. 157-180. [39]

OECD (2020), "First Meeting of the OECD Academic and Business Expert Advisory Group on Rural Innovation", OECD, Paris. [7]

OECD (2020), *Rural Well-being: Geography of Opportunities*, OECD Rural Studies, OECD Publishing, Paris, https://doi.org/10.1787/d25cef80-en. [1]

OECD (2020), "Second Meeting of the OECD Academic and Business Expert Advisory Group on Rural Innovation", OECD, Paris. [9]

OECD (2017), *The Geography of Firm Dynamics: Measuring Business Demography for Regional Development*, OECD Publishing, Paris, https://doi.org/10.1787/9789264286764-en. [20]

OECD (forthcoming), *Enhancing Innovation in Rural Regions: Scotland (UK)*, OECD Publishing, Paris. [37]

OECD (forthcoming), *Enhancing Innovation in Rural Regions: Switzerland*, OECD Publishing, Paris. [36]

OECD (n.d.), *Oslo Manual 2018*, OECD, Paris, https://www.oecd.org/sti/inno/oslo-manual-2018-info.pdf. [4]

OECD/Eurostat (2018), *Oslo Manual 2018: Guidelines for Collecting, Reporting and Using Data on Innovation, 4th Edition*, The Measurement of Scientific, Technological and Innovation Activities, OECD Publishing, Paris/Eurostat, Luxembourg, https://doi.org/10.1787/9789264304604-en. [3]

Pakes, A. and Z. Griliches (1980), "Patents and R&D at the firm level: A first report", *Economics Letters*, Vol. 5/4, pp. 377-381, https://doi.org/10.1016/0165-1765(80)90136-6. [8]

Rodríguez-Pose, A. and R. Fitjar (2013), "Buzz, Archipelago Economies and the Future of Intermediate and Peripheral Areas in a Spiky World", *European Planning Studies*, Vol. 21/3, pp. 355-372, https://doi.org/10.1080/09654313.2012.716246. [30]

Shearmur, R., C. Carrincazeaux and D. Doloreux (2016), *Handbook on the Geographies of Innovation*, Edward Elgar Publishing, https://doi.org/10.4337/9781784710774. [33]

Shearmur, R. and D. Doloreux (2016), "How open innovation processes vary between urban and remote environments: slow innovators, market-sourced information and frequency of interaction", *Entrepreneurship & Regional Development*, Vol. 28/5-6, pp. 337-357, https://doi.org/10.1080/08985626.2016.1154984. [32]

Simonen, J. and P. McCann (2010), "Knowledge transfers and innovation: The role of labour markets and R&D co-operation between agents and institutions", *Papers in Regional Science*, Vol. 89/2, pp. 295-309, https://doi.org/10.1111/j.1435-5957.2010.00299.x. [35]

Simonen, J. and P. McCann (2008), "Firm innovation: The influence of R&D cooperation and the geography of human capital inputs", *Journal of Urban Economics*, Vol. 64/1, pp. 146-154, https://doi.org/10.1016/j.jue.2007.10.002. [34]

Statistics Canada (2016), *Census of Population*, Statistics Canada Catalogue no. 98-400-X2016295. [29]

Taglioni, D. and D. Winkler (2016), "Making global value chains work for development", in *Making Global Value Chains Work for Development*, World Bank, Washington, DC, https://doi.org/10.1596/978-1-4648-0157-0_fm. [44]

Van Oort, F. (2017), *Urban Growth and Innovation: Spatially Bounded Externalities in the Netherlands*, Routledge. [40]

Wojan, T. and T. Parker (2017), *Innovation in the Rural Nonfarm Economy: Its Effect on Job and Earnings Growth, 2010-2014*, Economic Research Report No. (ERR-238), U.S. Department of Agriculture Economic Research Service. [15]

Notes

[1] Within OECD countries, the territorial classification of rural areas are often contingent on similar criteria including density and distances. However, each OECD country bases classifications on different cut-off points and it is not uncommon for ministries and departments within countries to not have a unified definition of rural. Often, classifications of rural areas are strongly determined by local policies and political agendas, such that the choice of using one definition over another has political implications. By using the harmonised OECD definition, the precision of rurality is not as accurate but we avoid issues arising from non-symmetrical incentives within countries.

[2] The OECD uses classification of administrative regions for territorial level analysis. Territorial level 2 (TL2) refer to large regions, while Territorial level 3 (TL3) refer to small regions. For European countries, they are aligned with the NUTS classification system of regions.

[3] In part, this was in order to overcome part of the sample size challenges associated with innovation surveys as well as the tangibility of outcomes associated with R&D investment and jobs.

[4] Hall (2015[41]) argues that "patent thickets" or heavily patented activities are associated with a reduction of patents for first time filers and increase for more technologically complex products. This type of anticompetitive behaviour raises entry costs that lead to less entry of firms into economic activities regardless of a firm's size. More recent research on regional innovation systems suggests that patents may not be as relevant for development as the literature currently suggests (Hall, 2020[42]).

[5] The headquarter bias refers to a measurement challenge where multi-plant enterprises that may have plants operating in different locations, but report all activity in one central location (usually at headquarters in large cities).

[6] In the case of R&D investment, while outcomes may change over time (benefits can perceived be in the short, medium or long term), input can be measured at a point in time and finds a premise to be territorially attributed to activity in the firm's headquarters. Another example is the use of patents. For example, patents that are developed at branches of different firms are often filed with the address of the firm's headquarters. While this is useful for legal reasons, it is clear that such measures systematically remove innovative activities from plants located outside of headquarter offices.

[7] Notwithstanding measurement critiques, it is hard to find alternatives with a good level of representativeness in rural areas. For this reason, survey-based data using the Oslo Manual's definition of innovation are a gold standard for understanding trends in innovation and its diffusion. However, in practice, for rural areas, the limited representativeness of this survey makes the use of such data close to impossible.

[8] California has several innovation hubs in addition to Silicon Valley that it draws from, including those at Silicon Beach and several research universities such as CalTech (including the NASA Jet Propulsion Laboratory campus), Stanford, UC Berkeley, UC Los Angeles and the other major University of California branches specialising in science (including maritime and agricultural research), IT and medical research universities.

[9] For more descriptions of the occupations that are identified as patentable, further information is available in Annex 3.D.

[10] The degree of rurality is an aggregate share value that captures the share of the population living outside of the FUA within each TL2. While it is a coarse indicator of rurality, it allows some classification on rurality.

[11] This is in line with trends in the rise of the new creative class, argued by Richard Florida (2002[38]) displayed in Annex Figure 3.F.1.

[12] Some authors refer to these forms of innovation as "slow innovation" and "reverse innovation", two types of innovation that occur more frequently in the periphery but are more difficult to capture in a comparable way in standard innovation statistics (Rodríguez-Pose and Fitjar, 2013[30]). Slow innovation refers to processes that do not quickly lose value over time (no rush to market) and develop more easily in peripheral areas (Mayer, 2020[31]). Such types of innovation take time to develop and are more dependent on non-market-sourced information (Shearmur and Doloreux, 2016[32]). Reverse innovation refers to innovations

in the periphery of the global business environment. Popularised in developing countries but relevant for local economies in industrialised areas, this type of innovation targets the production of new goods and services to the demands of local markets in rural regions. In some cases, it substitutes more expensive production costs with cheaper local alternatives from local value chains, while keeping most of the functionality. It captures marginal changes in production that are more targeted to local markets (Govindarajan and Euchner, 2012[43]; Taglioni and Winkler, 2016[44]).

4 Rural entrepreneurship and start-ups

This chapter focusing on characteristics of entrepreneurs and start-ups as a key component to promoting innovation in rural regions. It then focuses its analysis down to understanding characteristics of one class of innovative entrepreneur, young founders that may hinder or encourage start-up activity. Finally, it explores a counter-factual exercise that attempts to address whether differences in entrepreneurship rates among young founders are driven by individual socio-economic characteristics.

The traditional view of innovation is that it occurs in high-technology (high-tech) sectors but, as this report argues, that it comes in many forms. Some of the most relevant forms of innovations come from entrepreneurs that are considered "unicorns" (entrants that become high-growth firms), conduct disruptive activities (entrants that radically change incumbent competitor's business models) or build and innovate through marginal changes (entrants or incumbents that practice slow innovation). These types of new ("entrant") firms have tended to adopt best practices in product and process innovation to be competitive on the market.

According to research from the Future of Business Survey (OECD, n.d.[1]), start-ups in OECD countries account for approximately 14% of firms with a digital presence.[1] Entrepreneurs starting new endeavours have incentives to develop business models based on relatively new products and processes. While carving their place in the market, start-up entrepreneurs often need to find new and innovative ways of producing services and products for consumers. Understanding the conditions under which entrepreneurship occurs across regions is important for expanding our understanding of how to support innovation through entrepreneurship in rural regions.

What does innovative entrepreneurship look like in rural regions? The following section explores the basic characteristics of entrepreneurs and firms that innovate.

Firm dynamics and innovation potential for firms in rural regions

There is a strong potential for innovation through encouraging new entrepreneurship. In OECD countries, there is ample evidence suggesting that start-up entrepreneurs and small- and medium-sized enterprises (SMEs) tend to be innovative. A portion of start-ups are also highly productive (Freshwater et al., 2019[2]; Hall, 2011[3]; OECD, 2013[4]; 2019[5]). In addition, some evidence suggests that young founders are relatively innovative (Breschi, Lassébie and Menon, 2018[6]),[2] even if older entrepreneurs are prone to establishing high-growth firms (Azoulay et al., 2020[7]).

Higher start-up rates and creative destruction (firm churning, or firm birth and death rates), is often an indicator of healthy, evolving and innovative economies. In an OECD report (2017[8]) classifying regions into predominantly urban, intermediate or predominantly rural regions, firm dynamics are less active in predominantly rural regions as compared to predominantly urban regions. From the firm perspective, start-up rates are lower in predominantly rural regions (Figure 4.1).[3] One more firm per 1 000 workers is created in predominantly urban regions, as compared to predominantly rural regions. Low start-up rates in predominantly rural regions are symptomatic of barriers associated with framework conditions such as access to finance, supply chain and other resources and administrative burdens but may also reflect the sectoral or family-owned business characteristics that characterise rural economies.

A larger share of start-ups in predominantly rural regions operates in hospitality, industry and construction sectors than in predominantly urban regions (Figure 4.1).[4] These differences in sectors are not surprising. A relatively large hospitality sector is often associated with tourism and is often a feature of predominantly rural regions. For predominantly rural regions with access to natural resources and ecotourism, this is a substantial part of the economy.[5]

In predominantly rural regions, there are more new firm entrants (firm births) than closures (firm deaths). The opposite is true in predominantly urban regions, where more firms closed than started. In predominantly rural regions, 2 fewer firms per 1 000 workers closed, as compared to predominantly urban regions (Figure 4.1). While we cannot determine firm longevity with these statistics, lower firm death rates than births suggest relatively higher chances of firm survival. However, low firm death rates are an indicator of the market control of ageing firms, in particular for large firms in traditional sectors or sectors involving substantial investments. For instance, in Scotland (United Kingdom), there is evidence of ageing firms in rural areas distant from urban areas (OECD, forthcoming[9]). For rural regions, the fact that firms do not close as quickly signals longevity, which may be explained by less competition but also the size and sector of firms that dominate rural economies.

Figure 4.1. Birth and deaths of firms by sector and type of TL3 region

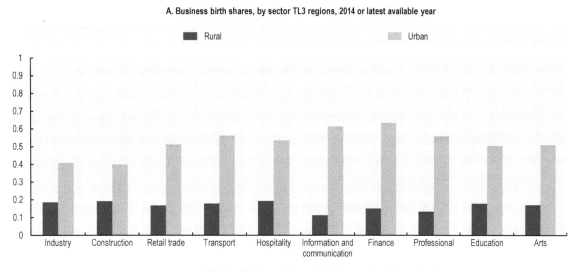

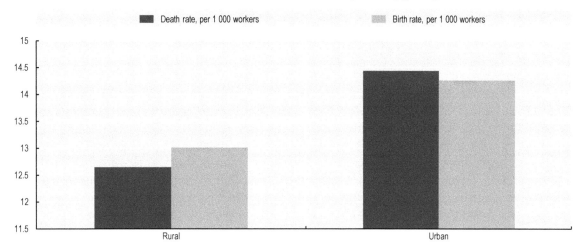

Note: Business births refer to the entrant of a new firm into the market. Business deaths refer to firm closures. The first figure displays the composition of business birth and death rates by type of region and by sector of economic activity of the firm (share of births and deaths in a sector as a proportion of total births in a region). The figures by regional typology are computed as averages across countries: Austria, the Czech Republic, Denmark, Estonia, Finland, France, Hungary, Ireland, Italy, Korea, the Netherlands, Norway, Poland, Portugal and the Slovak Republic. The data refer to 2014 or the last available year. All size classes are included. The second figure depicts the firm birth and death rates (births as a proportion of the number of employees in a region in the same year) by type of region. The typology used in the 3-tier urban/rural typology. The intermediate category is excluded to increase ease of interpretation. Averages are across all firms. The agricultural sector is not included.

Source: OECD (2017[8]), *The Geography of Firm Dynamics: Measuring Business Demography for Regional Development*, https://dx.doi.org/10.1787/9789264286764-en.

In sum, there are a number of takeaways. First, rates for starting new businesses in predominantly rural regions are lower. There is more than one missing start-up in predominantly rural regions as compared to predominantly urban regions. Second, firms and individuals in predominantly rural regions do not equally participate in the same sectors as those in predominantly urban areas. Predominantly rural regions tend to have a relatively higher share of the hospitality, manufacturing industry and construction sectors.[6] Last, there is lower dynamism in predominantly rural regions, as compared to predominantly urban regions, with lower birth and death rates of firms.

Young entrepreneurs and the potential for innovation in rural regions

Understanding drivers of innovation in rural regions involves understanding the conditions under which individuals decide to undertake a new endeavour. To understand entrepreneurship trends, the two sections below use microdata available in the European Union Labour Force Survey (EU-LFS). The analysis of firm dynamics uses a three-tiered typology on the degree of urbanisation from the European Commission that allows for some disaggregation but does not account for many of the heterogeneities between areas. To identify entrepreneurship, we used the question asking survey respondents whether they own their own firm. To determine start-up rates, we used both the questions of whether they own their own firm and whether they were also a firm owner in the previous year.[7] The data included is cross-sectional for 2011 and 2019, with recall variables to understand trends from the previous year. When all variables are available, the data cover OECD European countries including Austria, Belgium, Cyprus, the Czech Republic, Denmark, Estonia, Finland, Germany, Greece, Hungary, Iceland, Ireland, Italy, Lithuania, Latvia, Luxembourg, the Netherlands, Norway, Poland, Portugal, Spain, Sweden, Switzerland, Slovenia, the Slovak Republic and the United Kingdom. There are over 5 million observations distributed with over 2.7 million in 2011 and 2.4 million in 2019.

Supporting start-ups and entrepreneurship is often one of the objectives of innovation policy. Yet, there are missing entrepreneurs across all OECD countries. This is particularly a problem for youth and women (OECD/EU, 2019[10]; OECD, 2021[11]; OECD/EC, 2020[12]), where there is still substantial room to encourage the next generation of entrepreneurs. Using European Labour Force Survey data (EU-LFS) (Eurostat[13]) from 2019, the following section highlights determinants of young start-up entrepreneurship as a subset of highly innovative firms. The EU-LFS includes responses with available data from European countries[8] and is representative of activities in large economic sectors. The dataset contains a classification of large regions (TL2) and the degree of urbanisation classification including categories for rural areas, towns and suburbs and cities.[9] While not perfectly aligned, it allows for some level of analysis on a territorial level. For the purpose of this report, we consider a start-up entrepreneur as someone who reported owning their own firm in the current year but did not own a firm in the previous year. Following the literature review (Breschi, Lassébie and Menon, 2018[6]) and available characteristics of respondents, we consider the category of workers identified within the age groups 25-29 and 30-34 as young.

In 2019, there are 3 to 6 more entrepreneurs per 1 000 active individuals in rural areas as compared to cities, and towns and suburbs respectively.[10] This number indicates the relative importance of entrepreneurship in rural regions. However, the number of new entrepreneurs fell across all types of areas from 2011 to 2019. The relative decline was much stronger for rural areas. Rural areas lost 6 entrepreneurs per 1 000 active workers, while cities only 1 and towns and suburbs 3 (Figure 4.2). In context, these changes happen in European OECD countries that are still observing regional variation in growth rates following the global financial crisis. For rural and metropolitan regions, some of the challenges from the global financial crisis meant that they were systematically being left behind.

For understanding innovative entrepreneurship, one angle governments can take is to focus on the age category of entrepreneurs that are associated with relatively higher levels of innovation and growth. As elaborated previously, young start-up entrepreneurs have an increased probability of innovative activities. However, youth often make up a lower share of the rural and non-metropolitan regional economies. This is primarily due to regional migration factors that may encourage students to take up education opportunities in other regions. Bringing opportunities to rural regions for young start-up entrepreneurs can create a mechanism through which regional governments try to address depopulation issues related to youth migration patterns.

Figure 4.2. Young start-up entrepreneurs in 2011 and 2019

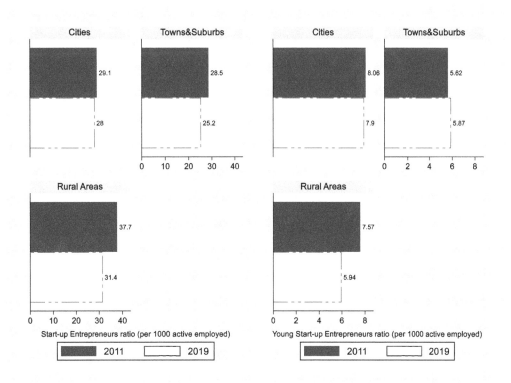

Note: Ratio of young (25-34 year-old) start-up entrepreneurs to active workforce (15-64) and degree of urbanisation categories. The sample includes Austria, Belgium, Cyprus, the Czech Republic, Denmark, Estonia, Finland, Germany, Greece, Hungary, Iceland, Ireland, Italy, Lithuania, Latvia, Luxembourg, the Netherlands, Norway, Poland, Portugal, Spain, Sweden, Switzerland, Slovenia, the Slovak Republic and the United Kingdom. There are over 5 million observations distributed with over 2.7 million in 2011 and 2.4 million in 2019. The analysis only includes individuals aged 15-64 who are actively employed. Weights for observations are based on yearly weighting factors in thousands of observations. $Startup\ ratios_{a,d,t} := Startup_{a,d,t}/Active\ Labour\ Force_{a,d,t}$

Source: Eurostat (n.d.[13]), *European Union Labour Force Survey (EU-LFS)*, https://ec.europa.eu/eurostat/web/microdata/european-union-labour-force-survey.

Young start-up entrepreneurs are struggling in rural regions. There are 2 missing young start-up entrepreneurs per 1 000 inhabitants in rural areas than in cities. There were 8 young start-up entrepreneurs in cities and only 6 in rural areas per 1 000 actively employed individuals in 2019, resulting in 25% fewer young start-up entrepreneurs. One in 125 young working-age individuals started firms in cities, whereas rural areas 1 in 133 young individuals create firms in 2019 (Figure 4.2). This is consistent with the trend of age-based demographic changes between territories. Combined with high levels of firm churning (start-ups and closures) observed in Figure 4.1, dense areas have a larger share of young entrepreneurs, which are more likely to use newer products and processes (Breschi, Lassébie and Menon, 2018[6]). As such the sed distribution of the active labour force population and more specifically, entrepreneurs, sheds light on the probability of innovating and the capacity for firms to innovate across different ographies.

There are close to 2 fewer young entrepreneurs per 1 000 active workers in European rural areas in 2019, as compared to 2011. This finding is temporally and spatially disproportionate since the share of young entrepreneurs stayed the same or grew marginally in cities and towns and suburbs (Figure 4.2). Rural areas lost close to 1 young entrepreneur per 500 active young individuals, the equivalent of the difference between rural areas and cities that is observed in 2019 (Figures 4.2 and 4.3). This comes in surprising contrast to the relatively high ratio of entrepreneurs in 2011. The change was similar for entrepreneurs between the ages of 30-34.[11] It is difficult to determine the cause of the trend. In addition to demographic change and migration, young working-age individuals move out of rural areas and there may be several other causes for this change including counter-cyclical policies and job scarcity.[12] For governments now addressing the impact of the COVID-19 pandemic, understanding start-up ecosystems for young entrepreneurs requires a territorial lens (OECD, 2021[14]).

Figure 4.3. Start-up entrepreneurs by age group, 2011 and 2019

Share of start-up entrepreneurs in the active labour force, by age category

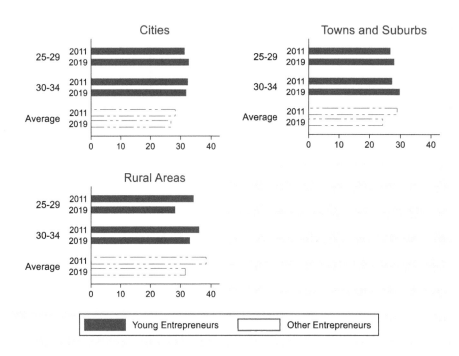

Note: Ratio of start-up entrepreneurs to active labour (15-64 years old) within age and degree of urbanisation categories. Averages exclude depicted young categories. The sample includes Austria, Belgium, Cyprus, the Czech Republic, Denmark, Estonia, Finland, Germany, Greece, Hungary, Iceland, Ireland, Italy, Lithuania, Latvia, Luxembourg, the Netherlands, Norway, Poland, Portugal, Spain, Sweden, Switzerland, Slovenia, the Slovak Republic and the United Kingdom. There are over 5 million observations: over 2.7 million in 2011 and 2.4 million in 2019. The analysis only includes individuals aged 15-64 who are actively employed. Observation weightings are based on yearly weighting factors in thousands of observations. $Startup\ ratios_{a,d,t} := Startup_{a,d,t} / Active\ Labour\ Force_{a,d,t}$
Source: Eurostat (n.d.[13]), *European Union Labour Force Survey (EU-LFS)*, https://ec.europa.eu/eurostat/web/microdata/european-union-labour-force-survey.

While entrepreneurship was growing in towns and suburbs and cities from 2011 to 2019, rural regions saw a 20% fall in entrepreneurs aged 25-29 and an 8% fall in entrepreneurs aged 30-34 (Figure 4.3). This is equivalent to a loss of 7 young entrepreneurs per 1 000 actively employed workers 25-29 years old as compared to cities, and 8 young entrepreneurs per 1 000 actively employed workers 25-29 years old as compared to towns and suburbs. Furthermore, there are 3 missing entrepreneurs per 1 000 actively employed workers between the ages of 30-34 as compared to cities and 6 missing entrepreneurs between the ages of 30-34 per 1 000 actively employed workers as compared to towns and suburbs. The decrease in young start-up entrepreneurship in rural areas is not observed in other areas. Focusing on building opportunities for young entrepreneurs who stay in rural regions is an important avenue for distributing the benefits of innovation. The sharp fall in the share of the youngest category of entrepreneurs in rural regions suggests that there may be room for improvement to focus on policies targeted at young entrepreneurs in rural areas and interlinkages between young entrepreneurs in rural areas and those in towns and suburbs.

On a regional level, regions with a higher degree of rurality tend to have higher ratios of young start-up entrepreneurs but there is no clear pattern between the size of the active labour force and young start-up entrepreneurship (TL2 regions, Figure 4.4). For the most part, the relationship between young start-up entrepreneurship and rurality is not clearly associated with the overall size of the regional active labour market.[13] Nevertheless, several regions demonstrate both high degrees of rurality and relatively high start-up entrepreneurship among young business owners.

- For example, Basilicata (ITF5) in Italy, with a relatively high degree of rurality, has a government that has taken steps to provide financial grants for SMEs to support innovative projects and technological adoption.
- In the Central Transdanubia (HU21) region of Hungary, innovative activities are diffused through foreign direct investment activities and structural funds to support R&D infrastructure building and investment in new technology.
- Other notable regions with high rates of young entrepreneurship and supportive framework conditions include the Friuli-Venezia Giulia region of Italy (ITH4), which contains incubators and a science park, and the Asturias in Spain (ES12), which was awarded the European Entrepreneurial Region award for its actions to support business entrepreneurship and growth, as well as access to finance and entrepreneurship education.

In sum, the findings from this section reflect trends in firm dynamics, entrepreneurship and young entrepreneurs in rural regions. While starting a new firm occurs more frequently in rural areas, there is still a relative decline in this activity. In rural areas, the drop in start-up entrepreneurship in the younger age categories is particularly exacerbated and outpaces the changes observed in other areas. Understanding the challenges of young entrepreneurs can help bring solutions for those interested in promoting rural and regional innovation and well-being.

Characteristics of young start-up entrepreneurs in rural areas

Socio-economic backgrounds matter for understanding entrepreneurship (Aghion et al., 2017[15]). Our analysis in this section debunks the conventional wisdom that start-up entrepreneurship is typically low in rural regions. There is evidence to suggest that lower start-up entrepreneurship rates in rural regions are primarily driven by socio-economic characteristics. The analysis initially draws its findings through regression analysis, followed by the application of a decomposition procedure that provides readers with a counterfactual exercise comparing rural areas and towns and suburbs to cities (see Annex B). It primarily uses labour force survey statistics from OECD countries in Europe. While the level of analysis is on an individual basis with over 5 million observations, the geographical typology of the analysis below is based on the degree of urbanisation. Geographies are grouped together to create two groups for the exercise.

Figure 4.4. Young start-up entrepreneurs in rural regions

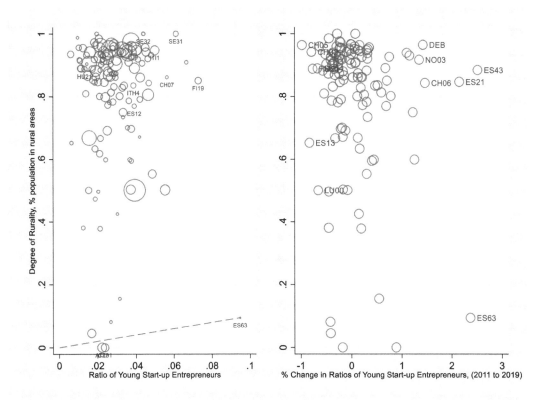

Note: The degree of rurality measures the share of the population that is identified as living in a non-metropolitan area within each TL2. Bubbles are weighed by the size of the active labour force.
Source: Eurostat (n.d.[13]), *European Union Labour Force Survey (EU-LFS)*, https://ec.europa.eu/eurostat/web/microdata/european-union-labour-force-survey, 2011 and 2019.

The counterfactual exercise first groups rural areas with towns and suburbs as the main group of interest, against those in cities. With these groupings, it helps us understand if all of the observable variables would be the same and whether the likelihood of a young person starting a firm would still be the same. To do this, the decomposition procedure:

- Provides an estimate of the differences in probability of becoming entrepreneurs between the two groups.
- Demonstrates what part of the probabilities are explained by observable variables (age, gender, education level, etc).
- Demonstrates whether the remaining differences between the two groups are statistically significant or simply false. To start this analysis, the rest of this section first runs simple linear probability regressions and then proceeds to the decomposition counterfactual.

As compared to young people living in cities, a young individual was 8.6% less likely to start a firm if they lived in a rural area (Figure 4.5, Panel A, and Table A B.1 in Annex B). While accounting for socio-economic, sector and country fixed effects, young individuals are significantly less likely to start firms if they live in rural areas. Comparatively, while young individuals in towns and cities may have also started fewer new firms, the data do not suggest the probability of young entrepreneurs starting new firms is significantly different from young entrepreneurs in cities. However, education levels and indicators of socio-economic welfare are important determinants of whether young individuals start firms and these characteristics often vary by territory (Figure 4.5).[14]

The main results of the regression analysis revealed a number of findings:

- **Unemployment is a major predictor of starting a firm for young entrepreneurs.** In the previous year, it is equally as important a determinant for start-up entrepreneurship in rural as in urban areas. However, this is driven by different factors in rural areas and more densely populated areas. Recent work by Navaretti and Markovic (2021[16]) suggests that firm-worker matches are less stable for younger employees in denser regions, suggesting that employee-firm sorting may have more longevity in rural regions (OECD, forthcoming[17]). Notwithstanding socio-economic characteristics of young entrepreneurs, unemployment in the previous year is a large and significant determinant of whether or not young entrepreneurs start a firm. Prior to controlling for socio-economic and territorial characteristics, young entrepreneurs were close to 60% likely to start a firm if they were not employed in the previous years. However, if we considered the likelihoods associated with other socio-economic factors such as education levels and living conditions, this probability jumped to close to the unitary value, meaning that young entrepreneurs in all types of regions do not leave jobs to start a company but rather start them after unemployment spells. Descriptively, young entrepreneurs in towns and suburbs may have a lower likelihood of starting a firm after unemployment than in other regions (Figure 4.5, Panel B) but, from the current evidence, it is not clear that the situation for young entrepreneurs is different from those in other areas.

- **Young rural entrepreneurs who start firms are more likely to still be looking for alternative sources of income and employment.** Indeed, rural entrepreneurs are more likely to simultaneously look for alternative jobs (although the significance of the correlation is weak). One explanation for this difference may be due to the expected returns from investing in entrepreneurship. If we assume that working nights and weekends is a proxy for motivation, then a positive correlation between starting a firm and working odd hours is indicative of strong incentives. Indeed, in Figure 4.5, working nights and weekends is positively associated with starting a firm as a young entrepreneur, and more so in rural regions. Young start-up entrepreneurs are more motivated in rural areas than in towns, suburbs and cities.

- **Young rural entrepreneurs have less access to training activities in the year prior to starting a firm.** Indeed, young entrepreneurs participating in training activities in the previous year are 43% more likely to start new firms. In cities, this probability increases to over 57%, while it drops to close to 26% in rural areas, towns and suburbs. While it is not possible to know the type of training a young entrepreneur receives with the available data, gaining skills in a variety of areas is nevertheless more likely to prepare entrepreneurs for the challenges of being a business owner.

- **Young rural start-up entrepreneurs tend to be more highly educated than their counterparts in cities, towns and suburbs.** Young rural individuals have a 44% higher chance of starting a firm if they have a post-secondary level of education as compared to those with primary levels of education and 30% more likely to start a firm if they have a secondary level of education. In comparison, in cities, young entrepreneurs only have a 30% higher likelihood of starting a firm given that they have a tertiary level of education and a 14% higher likelihood if they have a secondary level of education. As demonstrated in Figure 4.5, Panel B, as the education of the entrepreneur increases, so does the likelihood that they start a firm and the effect is greater if entrepreneurs live outside of cities. This trend could be either due to expected returns from entrepreneurship for highly educated individuals, limited opportunities for highly educated individuals in rural regions, or a mixture of both. To clarify this, we can look at unemployment and training trends that may indicate preparedness (Figure 4.5, Panel B).

- **Young rural individuals are motivated to start new firms,** by necessity, ingenuity, or a mix of the two (Baumol, 1990[18]). A large factor in the decision to become entrepreneurs may be necessity-based rather than choice-based or as a response to local labour market mismatch. Finding the motivations for such decisions is difficult. In one thought experiment, if this type of entrepreneurship was due to necessity, we would expect a positive and significant association between working at home and starting a company. This, however, is not clearly the case. There is a negative association between working at home and starting a company in cities, towns and suburbs, and rural areas. There is no clear evidence suggesting that the majority of young entrepreneurs are starting companies out of necessity (Figure 4.5, Panel B). Entrepreneurs in different geographical areas are not measurably different from each other in their likelihood to start firms after a year of unemployment.[15] The debate on this issue is not yet closed and there may be other interpretations of whether young entrepreneurs are creating firms out of necessity or out of ingenuity. However, it is important to consider that both types of entrepreneurship can lead to innovative outcomes, as long as one creates the correct opportunities for entrepreneurship.

  The evidence on training, education and motivation suggests that young start-up entrepreneurship in rural areas is in part due to a lack of alternative opportunities, in particular for the more highly educated cohorts. This is the case even if rural start-up entrepreneurs are more motivated than counterparts in other areas. For governments, the message from this analysis is that there is still a high demand for entrepreneurship opportunities in rural regions, whether it is due to a lack of alternatives or due to entrepreneurial motivation. To close the territorial gap, governments should support young entrepreneurs in their efforts to create opportunities in rural regions by removing barriers to opening firms and support for continued growth and development. Resources may be better allocated to reducing barriers to entrepreneurial growth and development in the local areas, while simultaneously focusing on providing skills and training to support entrepreneurs in rural regions.

- **Socio-economic backgrounds matter across territories.** Understanding parental education as a predictor of socio-economic background may help shed light on the household and socio-economic context of entrepreneurs. Parental education can be interpreted as a proxy for household socio-economic status, in particular when the young entrepreneur lives within the same household as the parents. In Figure 4.5, Panel B, we find that young entrepreneurs tend to have fathers with secondary education. If we assess this correlation by territorial type, we find that the relationship between fathers' education and entrepreneurship is only statistically significant for entrepreneurs in cities.

  A mother's education level, as a proxy for household socio-economic background, is particularly important for entrepreneurship in rural areas, towns and suburbs. In these areas, a young individual is 25% more likely to start a firm if they come from a household with a highly educated mother. Trends in the role of parents' education align with the assessment that entrepreneurship in rural areas is relatively more deliberate than in cities, and not out of necessity. If the father's education levels are closely tied to income and capital, as the literature suggests, then young entrepreneurs with family-based capital stock may be more deliberate in their entrepreneurial endeavours simply because they have relatively better access to resources, in particular if they start the company while living in the family household. Having a more educated mother (and, by proxy, with higher socio-economic status) may encourage children to pursue entrepreneurship in towns and suburbs.[16] Making public services more suitable for women entrepreneurs (including highly educated ones), for example by encouraging the adequate provision of quality childcare, adequate employment and entrepreneurship activities, safe neighbourhoods, affordable housing and better schools, increases entrepreneurial opportunities in rural areas, towns and suburbs. For governments, gender-blind territorial planning is a missed opportunity to reap the gains from the decades' worth of advances in gender equality.

Figure 4.5. Young start-up entrepreneurship probabilities, 2011 and 2019

A. Probability of starting a firm as a young entrepreneur, all areas, 2019

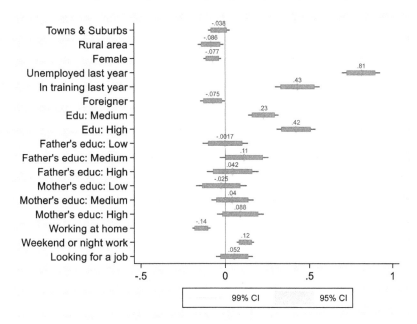

B. Probability of starting a firm as a young entrepreneur by area, 2011 and 2019

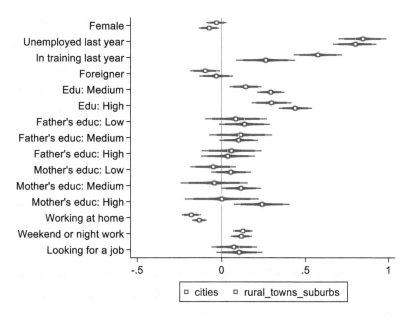

Note: Unreported controls include occupation (ISCO - International Standard Classification of Occupations), sector (NACE - Nomenclature of Economic Activities) and country fixed effects. The base groups for each categorical variable are as follows: cities for territorial indicators; low education for education level; and father or mother not living in the same household for the educational level of parents. Standard errors are clustered at the regional level (TL2). Confidence Intervals are reported at the 95% and 99% levels.

Source: Eurostat (n.d.[13]), *European Union Labour Force Survey (EU-LFS)*, https://ec.europa.eu/eurostat/web/microdata/european-union-labour-force-survey.

- **Young foreigners are less likely to start firms in cities, as compared to rural areas, towns and suburbs.** While the likelihood of becoming a young entrepreneur is 7.5% lower for foreigners as compared to natives, this is mostly driven by foreigners in cities. In rural areas, towns and suburbs, this difference is negligible. Evidence from the perspective of the United States suggests that there are strong hubs of immigrant entrepreneurship (in some cases with over 40% of new firms being started by migrants) in some densely populated areas, such as California, New York and New Jersey. These are often also associated with high levels of innovation (Pekkala Kerr and Kerr, 2020[19]). The academic literature on innovation, entrepreneurship and migration often finds that foreigners positively contribute to innovation and the transfer of new knowledge and expertise (Azoulay et al., 2020[20]; OECD, forthcoming[21]). Increasing the flow of migrant entrepreneurs and opportunities for entrepreneurship among foreigners can provide an avenue for improving dynamism and innovation diffusion in local markets. While further analysis is needed to understand the type of migrants that are most prone to innovative entrepreneurship in rural areas, migrant integration and assimilation policies that encourage foreign settlement in less dense areas are likely to bring a variety of skills and capital that encourages entrepreneurship and innovation ecosystem.

- **Last, young female entrepreneurship is lagging, particularly in towns, suburbs and rural regions**. Many factors impact young female entrepreneurship, including access to formal and informal networks, financial capital, human capital and government resources (OECD, 2021[11]). The qualitative findings align with quantitative findings that suggest that young women are less likely to start companies in particular in towns and suburbs (Figure 4.5 and Table A B.1 in Annex B).

Young women in rural areas, towns and suburbs tend to start more firms when they are more highly educated (Figure 4.6). While young men also tend to start firms when they are more educated, education is less of a predictor of starting a firm for men than it is for women. In rural areas, towns and suburbs, women tend to have higher levels of education than their male counterparts. The higher her educational attainment, the more likely she is to become an entrepreneur in rural areas. If women in rural areas, towns and suburbs have a tertiary level of education, they are 55% more likely to start a firm than if they had a low level of education. For men, this number is lower at 27.5%. Women are more likely to start a firm while working from home and anecdotally tend to have a different sectoral focus in business endeavours, for instance in service and hospitality sectors that have a higher share of rural economies and lower wages. Female entrepreneurship, like male entrepreneurship, is dependent on access to capital and labour resources, in addition to the quality of public services and welfare policies. Focusing on levelling the playing field in the opportunities for men and women, by providing adequate public sector support for female entrepreneurship and encouraging entrepreneurship across all sectors, is an important step in encouraging female entrepreneurship in productive and transitioning sectors.

In sum, young entrepreneurs are 8.5% less likely to start a firm if they live in rural areas. This penalty is majorly determined by training and education opportunities, as well as socio-economic characteristics of young people, including with migrant status, and their parents. Women are at a particular disadvantage as having a higher (post-secondary) level of education is a stronger determinant than for men. Last, unemployment may be a high motivator for starting a new firm and those that set up a business in cities, often have better access to education and training, providing them with an advantage in their entrepreneurial journey.

Figure 4.6. Gender differences in young entrepreneurship rates, towns, suburbs and rural areas, 2011 and 2019

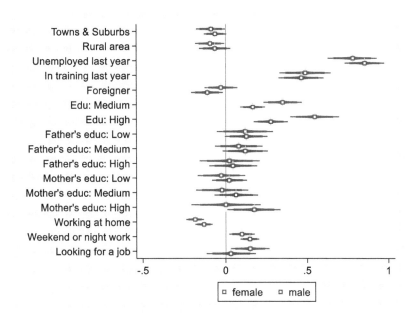

Note: Unreported controls include occupation (ISCO), sector (NACE), year and country fixed effects. The base groups for each categorical variable are as follows: cities for territorial indicators; low education for education level; and father or mother not living in the same household for the educational level of parents. Standard errors are clustered at the regional level (TL2). Confidence Intervals are reported at the 95% and 99% levels. Observations in cities are excluded from these regressions. This table excludes individuals living in cities.

Source: Eurostat (n.d.[13]), *European Union Labour Force Survey (EU-LFS)*, https://ec.europa.eu/eurostat/web/microdata/european-union-labour-force-survey.

Understanding alternative scenarios for young entrepreneurs in rural areas

It is important to understand the degree to which differences in entrepreneurship rates are due to individual characteristics or the general ecosystem of the entrepreneurial environment. This section of the report examines this question through a counterfactual exercise by separating the part of the analysis that contributes to observable differences versus those that are attributed to unknown factors. These unknown factors may be related to different framework conditions outside of the control of the young individuals. To counterbalance this, we can generate a counterfactual analysis that projects scenarios where observable characteristics are equivalent. One such method is the Oaxaca-Blinder decomposition, further explained in Annex 3.A, which decomposes differences in outcome variables between two groups as belonging to observable and non-observable characteristics. For the purpose of measurement and statistical power, and in line with the counterfactual model, the analysis needs to be split into two groups. While rural areas are often more remote than towns and suburbs, much of the policy literature assesses parts of towns and cities as being relatively more akin to rural areas than to cities. Therefore, for this part of the analysis, rural areas are grouped with towns and suburbs.

The decomposition analysis in Figure 4.7 demonstrates that, when controlling for observable factors, the difference between entrepreneurship probability in cities versus rural areas, towns and suburbs is small and close to 0.2% (meaning rural areas have a 0.2% lower chance). The difference between the two groups is significant. Around half of the difference is explained by observable characteristics like education, gender, training, parents' education (and by proxy socio-economic status), migration status and whether they are working from home or the office, or if they work nights and weekends. Once we control for these characteristics, there remains a large share of unexplained factors that impact the decision to start new firms.

Figure 4.7. Decomposition of the probability of becoming a young start-up entrepreneur

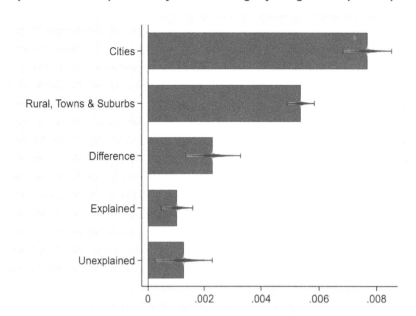

Note: Controls include sector, occupation and country fixed effects. All standard errors are clustered at the regional (TL2) level. Confidence intervals are reported at the 95% and 99% levels. The coefficients are the following: cities 0.0077; rural areas, towns and suburbs 0.0053665; difference 0.0023; explained 0.0010; and unexplained 0.0013. All estimates are significant at the 95% confidence level. All coefficients are also significant at the 99% confidence interval.
Source: Eurostat (n.d.[13]), *European Union Labour Force Survey (EU-LFS)*, https://ec.europa.eu/eurostat/web/microdata/european-union-labour-force-survey.

Socio-economic factors explain half of the territorial disparity. If entrepreneurs in rural areas and towns and suburbs had the same socio-economic profiles and sectoral and regional attributes,[17] the gap between the probability of becoming a start-up entrepreneur would drop by close to 50%.

The message from this analysis is twofold. First, individuals in less dense areas are hindered by having a different set of opportunities than those in cities. Second, ensuring equal access to public services including educational opportunities or other regional framework conditions is an important aspect of encouraging entrepreneurial dynamism associated with innovation, but there is still more to be done to level the playing field.

The explained portion of the analysis is useful for targeting a few key policy areas where governments can begin to address how to reduce the gaps between less dense areas and cities. However, half of the difference between entrepreneurial rates for young people remains unexplained and is likely attributed to rural-specific factors or challenges. These can include, among others, barriers to entrepreneurship due to access to finance, labour, physical and digital markets and government services and linkages within and between the local economy and other areas, as well as regional attributes.[18]

Access to education and access to digital infrastructure are two increasingly important framework conditions for rural innovation. For example, expanding access to quality education from a young age, vocational education opportunities and entrepreneurial training services are particularly relevant to ensure equal opportunities to participate and benefit from rural innovation. Furthermore, enabling access to quality and affordable digital infrastructure is increasingly important in a digitalised economy both for economic growth but also for access to digital education and health services (OECD, 2021[22]; forthcoming[23]).

In sum, the penalty associated with young entrepreneurs in rural areas, towns and suburbs, exists and is statistically significant. However, for the large part, it is explained by socio-economic differences and sectoral and regional attributes. What remains is likely explained by various framework conditions, networking spill-overs and regional aspects that are not easily captured in the model.

References

Aghion, P. et al. (2017), *The Social Origins of Inventors*, National Bureau of Economic Research, Cambridge, MA, https://doi.org/10.3386/w24110. [15]

Azoulay, P. et al. (2020), "Age and high-growth entrepreneurship", *American Economic Review: Insights*, Vol. 2/1, pp. 65-82, https://doi.org/10.1257/aeri.20180582. [7]

Azoulay, P. et al. (2020), *Immigration and Entrepreneurship in the United States*, National Bureau of Economic Research, Cambridge, MA, https://doi.org/10.3386/w27778. [20]

Baumol, W. (1990), "Entrepreneurship: Productive, unproductive, and destructive", *Journal of Political Economy*, Vol. 98/5, pp. 893–921, https://www.jstor.org/stable/2937617. [18]

Breschi, S., J. Lassébie and C. Menon (2018), "A portrait of innovative start-ups across countries", *OECD Science, Technology and Industry Working Papers*, No. 2018/2, OECD Publishing, Paris, https://doi.org/10.1787/f9ff02f4-en. [6]

Eurostat (n.d.), *European Union Labour Force Survey (EU-LFS)*, European Union, https://ec.europa.eu/eurostat/web/microdata/european-union-labour-force-survey. [13]

Freshwater, D. et al. (2019), "Business development and the growth of rural SMEs", *OECD Regional Development Working Papers*, No. 2019/07, OECD Publishing, Paris, https://doi.org/10.1787/74256611-en. [2]

Hall, B. (2011), "Innovation and productivity", National Bureau of Economic Research, Cambridge, MA, https://doi.org/10.3386/w17178. [3]

Navaretti, G. and B. Markovic (2021), "Place-based policies and the foundations of productivity in the private sector". [16]

OECD (2021), *Entrepreneurship Policies through a Gender Lens*, OECD Studies on SMEs and Entrepreneurship, OECD Publishing, Paris, https://doi.org/10.1787/71c8f9c9-en. [11]

OECD (2021), *Implications of Remote Working Adoption on Place Based Policies: A Focus on G7 Countries*, OECD Publishing, Paris, https://doi.org/10.1787/b12f6b85-en. [14]

OECD (2021), *Policies for Present and Future Service Delivery Across Territories*, OECD, Paris. [22]

OECD (2019), *Measuring the Digital Transformation: A Roadmap for the Future*, OECD Publishing, Paris, https://doi.org/10.1787/9789264311992-en. [5]

OECD (2017), *The Geography of Firm Dynamics: Measuring Business Demography for Regional Development*, OECD Publishing, Paris, https://doi.org/10.1787/9789264286764-en. [8]

OECD (2013), *OECD Science, Technology and Industry Scoreboard 2013: Innovation for Growth*, OECD Publishing, Paris, https://doi.org/10.1787/sti_scoreboard-2013-en. [4]

OECD (forthcoming), *Enhancing Innovation in Rural Regions: Scotland (UK)*, OECD Publishing, Paris. [9]

OECD (forthcoming), *Enhancing Innovation in Rural Regions: United States*, OECD Publishing, Paris. [23]

OECD (forthcoming), *The Contribution of Migration to Regional Development*, OECD, Paris. [21]

OECD (n.d.), *The Future of Business Survey*, OECD, Paris, https://www.oecd.org/sdd/business-stats/the-future-of-business-survey.htm. [1]

OECD (forthcoming), "The Spatial Dimensions of Private Sector Productivity", OECD, Paris. [17]

OECD/EC (2020), "Policy brief on recent developments in youth entrepreneurship", *OECD SME and Entrepreneurship Papers*, No. 19, OECD Publishing, Paris, https://doi.org/10.1787/5f5c9b4e-en. [12]

OECD/EU (2019), *The Missing Entrepreneurs 2019: Policies for Inclusive Entrepreneurship*, OECD Publishing, Paris, https://doi.org/10.1787/3ed84801-en. [10]

Pekkala Kerr, S. and W. Kerr (2020), "Immigrant entrepreneurship in America: Evidence from the survey of business owners 2007 & 2012", *Research Policy*, Vol. 49/3, p. 103918, https://doi.org/10.1016/j.respol.2019.103918. [19]

Notes

[1] This refers to the unweighted average of shares of companies that have been incorporated less than one year ago and have a media presence (Facebook page). The statistic is the average of four months including December 2017, January, February and April 2018. The survey was not conducted in March 2018. The data were collected on a monthly basis from 2016 to 2018 as part of the Future of Business Survey collaboration between Facebook, OECD and the World Bank.

[2] Using a database of start-ups (Crunchbase) and patent data, Breschi, Lassébie and Menon (2018[6]) find that firms with founders between the ages of 28 and 33 tend to be more innovative. This is the basis for the age categories used to focus the analysis on characteristics of innovative entrepreneurs.

[3] From the perspective of individual entrepreneurs, predominantly rural regions also suffer from relatively lower entrepreneurs than predominantly urban regions (Figure 4.3).

[4] Unfortunately, comparable data sources that include the agricultural sector are not available.

[5] It is also notable that due to data limitations, the agricultural sector, an activity in predominantly rural and intermediate regions, is often omitted from such analysis.

[6] The analysis unfortunately excludes the agricultural sector, which is often more dominantly represented in rural regions.

[7] There is room to assess that some ownership may be related to mergers, or family acquisitions, however, at least for young individuals, this is this less often a concern. It remains an approximate indicator of

start-up entrepreneurship that allows some socio-economic analysis that may, in other cases, require more complicated and less comparable harmonisation of employee-employer databases across countries.

[8] The countries in the survey that contained sufficient variables for this analysis included the Czech Republic, Estonia, Germany, Greece, Hungary, Latvia, Lithuania, Norway, Portugal, the Slovak Republic and Spain.

[9] Eurostat's degree of urbanisation in the 2019 EU-LFS categorises areas based on the 2011 population grid and the 2016 local administrative unit (LAU) boundaries. It classifies areas based on the share of local population living in urban clusters and urban centres, LAUs or communes into three types of areas: cities (densely populated areas), towns and suburbs (intermediate density areas) and rural areas (sparsely populated areas). All statistics using the EU-LFS are weighted population estimates.

[10] Entrepreneurial ratios per 1 000 working-age individuals for 2019 are 29 in cities, 28.5 in towns and suburbs and 31.4 in rural areas. Start-up rates in this analysis is based on the proportion of entrepreneurs who were not business owners in the previous year. From the perspective of business owners in the labour force statistics, any differences between start-up rates using labour force data and those using firm data may reflect different trends in multiple-owner firms, or due to the sample of countries included in each of the databases.

[11] More analysis of the motivation of the different types of entrepreneurship will be explored in subsequent sections.

[12] The relatively high levels of rural young entrepreneurs in 2011, right in the aftermath of the global financial crisis, may reflect entrepreneurship as an obligation – for example, in the face of low scarce job opportunities – rather than a choice. If entrepreneurship by obligation leads to entrepreneurship in saturated markets, this suggests that this type of entrepreneurship may not necessarily be as innovative. Alternatively, the high level of entrepreneurship in 2011 and drop in 2019, may reflect the medium- and long-run distributional impacts of the Global Financial Crisis creating an environment where firm ownership is riskier and potential entrepreneurs are hesitant.

[13] This is captured by the markers weighted by the size of the labour force in left panel of Figure 4.4. While the relationship is noisy, assessing rurality within TL2 regions allows for incorporating intermediate areas more akin to rural regions than cities into the analysis.

[14] A mother's education level, as a proxy for household socio-economic background, is particularly important for entrepreneurship in rural areas, towns and suburbs. In these areas, a young individual is 25% more likely to start a firm if they come from a household with a highly educated mother.

[15] In a linear probability (probit) model with interaction terms on previous year unemployment and degree of urbanisation, estimation results were not significant for any interactions.

[16] In a fertility- and household-decision-making context, more educated women may decide to have more children only outside of dense cities (or rural areas). With increasing rates of female educational attainment over the past decades and the household decision-making choices of more educated mothers tending to favour human capital investment in children, the growth of female education in previous decades is continuing to have an impact on intergenerational outcomes.

[17] These include gender, unemployment status, education levels, socio-economic background, motivation, industry, occupation and more general attributes associated with regions (regional fixed effects).

[18] These do not refer to regional characteristics. If we exclude regional level effects that often capture time-invariant macro-economic framework conditions, the decomposition shows a much higher level of differences between the two groups that remains unexplained.

5 Innovation as a driver of opportunities for rural regions

This chapter first discusses the important role that social innovation plays for rural development. It then examines the effects of innovation on several dimension of well-being including on employment, productivity, household income and inequality in rural regions.

The association between innovation, long-term growth and productivity is well established, but its impact on economic and social outcomes is more nuanced and analysis within countries and for rural regions is far more limited. For example, innovation in the public sector is often attributed to improvements in the reach of public services to more remote areas, such as e-health and e-education but can lead to increasing disparities, which was the case during the COVID-19 crisis (Markey, Ryser and Halseth, 2020[1]; OECD, 2021[2]; 2020[3]). In the short and medium terms, product and process innovation can result in the loss of jobs and income, increase the polarisation of jobs and inequality between frontier and lagging firms, and regions (Acemoglu and Restrepo, 2020[4]; Akcigit, Grigsby and Nicholas, 2017[5]; Goos, Manning and Salomons, 2009[6]; 2014[7]; Greenan, 2003[8]; Thesmar and Thoenig, 2000[9]; OECD, 2016[10]). However, in the midst of growing fears of how the acceleration of human-replacing innovations affects workers, innovation still has the possibility of transforming opportunities for our economies (Autor, 2014[11]).

The next part of the analysis focuses on outcomes associated with innovation and explores how social innovation is critical for rural areas. It then delves into associated outcomes on a regional level and concludes with more precise information from case studies. The analysis relies on data from the European Union Labour Force Survey (EU-LFS), OECD regional statistics and national sources of data. Rurality is defined as the share of rural populations based on large (TL2) regions.

Social innovation in rural regions

An important aspect of living in rural regions is initiatives that combine new and improved methods of delivering goods and services that have a social purpose. Often these types of innovation are not directly measurable but are increasingly growing in importance for policy makers. The outcome of social innovators often directly contributes to local welfare and increased provision of public services.

It is increasingly clear that societal challenges such as climate change cannot be addressed solely by one actor or through traditional governmental top-down responses. In this perspective, rural areas appear particularly challenged often due to limited financial resources, demographic change, infrastructure and availability of public services such as healthcare, transportation or access to education. Social innovation is seen as an opportunity to support social well-being, tackle marginalisation and trigger transformative changes through collective action; it can reduce social inequalities and disproportionate resource use and promote sustainable development.

The working definition of social innovation adopted within the framework of the OECD Forum on Social Innovations was that it "can concern conceptual, process or product change, organisational change and changes in financing, and can deal with new relationships with stakeholders and territories" (OECD, 2000[12]). The OECD definition clearly links social innovation to local development, as social innovation is seen as a way to improve the welfare of individuals and communities and explicit reference is made to new relationships with territories (OECD, 2000[12]). The research underlines that because social innovation responds to place-based challenges, it is sometimes difficult for these initiatives to grow beyond the community. It is typically locally embedded and its conditions can vary from one territory to another.

There are many examples where local action groups tackle issues of social exclusion and promote co-operative entrepreneurship or application of new digitalisation tools in rural areas.[1] Social innovation responds to challenges in a rural context:

- *By activating the power of collective knowledge* involving various stakeholders, it identifies innovative ways of addressing societal challenges. Local actors, such as civil society, businesses or local government could work together with the objective to find novel practices to address specific local challenges; often these solutions involve new social relationships and collaborations, participative governance mechanisms along with economic opportunities.

- *By developing resilient and sustainable solutions* as a result of the alignment of multiple interests of various stakeholders towards a common goal. This leads to positive systemic change, especially in marginalised rural areas, which must reinvent their role and their capacity to innovate.

- *By increasing a sense of belonging to a local area and community* as well as a desire to prevent excessive emigration through finding solutions to local challenges and creating more vibrant and active rural societies (Zivojinovic, Ludvig and Hogl, 2019[13]).

- *By improving the impact and value for money* through finding alternative ways to deliver the same service and especially by introducing preventive approaches, social innovation addresses the issue of limited financial resources and cuts future costs by explicitly reducing the negative externalities of economic activities.

There is momentum for change in rural areas through social innovation. Until recently, the prevailing view was that not all local contexts are capable of nurturing social innovation (Moulaert et al., 2014[14]), suggesting that social innovation is more likely to happen in urban areas. However, a growing number of academics argue the contrary and find momentum in rural areas (Aldea-Löppönen, 2011[15]; Bock, 2016[16]; Lindberg and Jansson, 2016[17]; Neumeier, 2017[18]), in particular thanks to the progressive advancement of digitalisation and novel practices (Christmann, 2017[19]). Examples include homecare or online training, which have particularly been picked up during the COVID-19 crisis, as well as rural mobility solutions through an e-car sharing initiative in a village in Germany (Dorfmobil Barsikow, 2020[20]). The outcome of social innovators often directly contributes to improved local welfare and more efficient provision of public services. The OECD paper "Building local ecosystems for social innovation: A methodological framework" (2021[21]) explores the approach to enhance the capacity of social innovation at the local level, to grow, scale as well as develop evidence-based policies around this subject.

The quality and diversity of the social innovation community constitute the basis for the success of the social innovation ecosystem in a particular territory. Community is built by the actors of social innovation, including the private sector, public sector and civil society organisations, which can comprise a variety of social economy players and citizens who play different and interchanging roles in the initiation and development of social innovations. This multi-stakeholder perspective is crucial for social innovation and helps to reinvent the traditional roles of the actors. For example, civil society actors – such as associations or citizens – are often taking the lead in the process of initiation (as well as development) of social innovation because their missions are strongly associated with social or environmental purposes (Bekker et al., 2013[22]).

The presence of active civil society in a territory and a relatively higher density of civil society could indicate a higher propensity for initiation of social innovations. Specifically, in rural areas, research (Jungsberg et al., 2020[23]) on social innovation refers to civil society as the most important actors during the social innovation initiation phase, even if they are often less present in rural areas (see Figure 5.1). Social entrepreneurs (Richter et al., 2019[24]) or older people (Noack and Federwisch, 2020[25]) are also specifically highlighted by some researchers as particularly active sub-groups in relation to rural social innovation. Similar to the distribution of the labour force in different territories, in European countries, close to 20% of employment in associations is located in rural regions, with close to 30% in towns and suburbs. Nevertheless, the share of individuals working in associations as a primary occupation is only marginally lower in rural areas, as compared to towns, suburbs and cities. Understanding employment in association shares alone is not sufficient for capturing the growing importance of social innovation in rural areas but allows us to provide at least a relative understanding of some types of social innovation. The growing importance of social innovation makes it necessary to explore ways how metrics can be applied in order to measure it and in order to analyse ways to overcome the narrow focus of metrics on economic-only issues.

Figure 5.1. Employment in associations

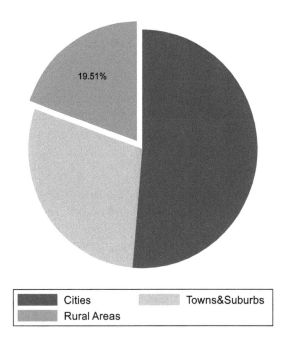

Note: Share of individuals employed in Nomenclature of Economic Activities (NACE) categories Arts, Entertainment and Recreation (R) and Other Service Activities (S) in a first or second job.
Source: Eurostat (n.d.[26]), *European Union Labour Force Survey (EU-LFS)*, https://ec.europa.eu/eurostat/web/microdata/european-union-labour-force-survey, 2018 or the latest available data.

Social innovation is a source of new arrangements and co-operation modes for specific regions and rural areas. One such example is the region of Navarra, Spain, one of the pioneers of promoting social innovation over recent years. The region has put a number of initiatives in place to promote social innovation. The Social Innovation Unit was created in 2017 as an important action under the government of Navarra's Integral Plan for Social Economy 2017-2020. The unit's first output was a dedicated ecosystem for social innovation with a customised methodology at the local level which promoted over 35 local social innovation projects, including initiatives to improve the quality of food in schools and access to health via online services in rural areas. Another example is Coompanion Blekinge, Sweden, which works with the local county government, acting as a co-operatively owned intermediary with public funding and 25 physical sites that support for-profit or non-profit initiatives that serve a social purpose (OECD, forthcoming[27]).

In sum, social innovation is an increasingly recognised form of innovation building on the specific attributes of local economies, in particular where access to public services is lacking. However, the quality and diversity of the social innovation community constitute the basis for the success of the social innovation ecosystem in a particular territory. Finally, the presence of an active civil society in a territory could indicate a higher propensity for the initiation of social innovations.

Effects of innovation on several dimensions of well-being in rural regions

This report has identified several reasons why we should reconsider our understanding of innovation and its drivers in rural regions. In the following section, the analysis estimates the effects of innovation on employment, productivity, productivity growth, household income and indicators of regional income inequality (Gini index). The report uses a two-step regression analysis depicted in Figure 5.2 to explore changes in observable characteristics over the 2000 to 2019 period for OECD countries as they are associated with innovation. Further details of the regression analysis are provided in Tables A C.1 and A C.2 of the Annex. In this instance, innovation is proxied through population-weighted patent intensity indicators and outcomes are variables taken from the OECD Regional Database. Unfortunately, data on relevant occupations was not available across all TL2 regions. As a first step, working on analysis on a TL2 level requires accounting for the degree of rurality using shares of non-metropolitan populations within large TL2 regions. While it is less preferable than analysis on a level of small regions (TL3), it allows for wider usage of available controls and statistics. As such, the analysis focuses on a two-tail analysis that ranks TL2 regions by the degree of rurality and categorises two groups, those whose shares of non-metropolitan populations are less than the 25th percentile of regions and those above the 75th percentile of regions that identifies TL2 regions as having a relatively high share of non-metropolitan populations.

Regions with relatively higher shares of non-metropolitan populations observe a positive correlation between innovation and real household income, elderly dependency ratios, population density and population density growth[2] (as observed in the first and seventh column of Tables A C.1 and A C.2 of the Annex). When using patent ratios (patents per population employed in high-technology [high-tech] industry) to proxy innovation, trends in regions with relatively higher density and those with relatively lower density are similar for all the same variables except for population density growth. This finding is not surprising, as growth in populations increases opportunities for innovative interactions in formalised settings. For regions with relatively more rural characteristics, the demographic challenge remains a key factor in creating the environment for innovation.

Considering the first step, innovation is associated with increases in employment, productivity, household income and growth in productivity in the following year (Figure 5.2). The trends related to key outcomes of interest for policy makers suggest that pursuing policies focused on increasing innovative activities in rural regions has a relatively stronger response for areas with more rural characteristics than in more dense regions, at least in the first year. This is in line with the literature on innovation and short-term outcomes. Given the arguments made in the first part of the chapter about occupational structure, we expect this outcome to be lower-end observations.

The benefits of innovative activities are stronger for regions with more rural characteristics. In Figure 5.2, the benefits of innovation to employment in areas with more rural characteristics are higher than in denser regions by a factor of 5.5. A one-unit increase in the ratio of patents to population results in a twofold increase in employment for a high share of individuals living in non-metropolitan regions, while it only results in a 40% increase in employment for individuals living in regions with the least share of non-metropolitan populations. Household incomes increase by 86% in regions with a relatively high share of non-metropolitan populations, while they increase by 30% in regions with relatively fewer non-metropolitan populations. A one-unit increase in patent intensity is associated with a 91% increase in productivity in regions with relatively high shares of non-metropolitan populations. This impact is lower, at 54%, in regions with a lower share of non-metropolitan populations. Furthermore, productivity growth (value-added per worker) is also positively associated with increased intensity of innovation and patenting activities, and relatively stronger for areas with larger shares of non-metropolitan populations. The higher level of impact for rural regions suggests that there may be larger gains to innovation, traditional or otherwise, in areas with higher shares of non-metropolitan populations that can help bridge the geography of discontent.

However, innovation is a precursor to inequality in the short run for all regions. High-tech innovation breeds inequality in the short run in both rural and dense settings. A one-unit increase in the patent intensity results in an 11% increase in wage inequality (Gini indicator) in regions with higher shares of non-metropolitan populations but only a 3% increase in wage inequality in areas with lower shares of non-metropolitan populations. The estimates demonstrate that patent-based innovation is a precursor to higher levels of inequality in rural areas than in denser settings. But this should be observed with caution. Using measures of innovation through patenting (creation) cannot capture the wage impacts of the adoption of innovative goods and services in industries that more accurately capture the rural economy. There is a further avenue to understand what types of innovation lead to increases in inequality versus those that are more distributive.

Figure 5.2. Effects of innovation on inequality, productivity, productivity growth, income and employment

Comparison between regions with various degrees of rurality, 2000-19

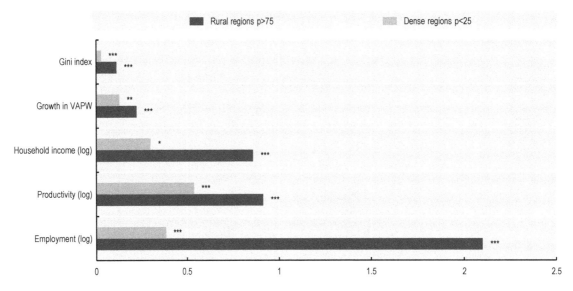

Note: Rural regions (p>75) refer to TL2 regions that are characterised as regions above the 75th percentile of the TL2 rurality index. Dense regions are TL2 regions with a degree of rurality that is less than the 25th percentile of all TL2 regions. Values include linear projections for years with missing values. VAPW refers to value-added per worker. The output in the figure is the result of a two-step least-squared fixed effects model estimating the impact of a one-unit change in the ratio of patents to the population on various outcome variables using the variation of aggregate statistics from previous years. The first-step estimation model is a fixed effects model on the level of TL2 with lagging independent variables. The second-step estimation captures the variation in outcome variables, which is explained by the patent-per-population innovation proxy. Controls include lags and shares in gross value added and employment in each major NACE sector. F-tests for instruments are above 10 and all are statistically significant to the 0.001 level. They are reported in Tables A C.1 and A C.2 of the Annex. The symbols in the graph correspond to the following: *** $p<0.01$, ** $p<0.05$, * $p<0.1$.
Source: OECD (n.d.[28]), *OECD Regional Demography (database)*, https://stats.oecd.org/Index.aspx?DataSetCode=REGION_DEMOGR.

In sum, innovation is important for long-term growth, jobs and welfare outcomes. However, outcomes are not the same across regions. In general, regions with the highest shares of non-metropolitan populations tend to have a more positive link between increased innovation intensities than others. This finding suggests that there is a relatively larger opportunity for growth through innovation in regions with more non-metropolitan populations than regions with a smaller share of less non-metropolitan populations. Second, welfare-enhancing innovation is not automatic. While there is a positive correlation between real household income and innovation in regions with a higher share of non-metropolitan populations in the short run, there is also a larger increased association with growing inequalities.

Conclusions

The report sets the scene for establishing a framework for understanding innovation in rural areas through a rural lens, explores how to promote a relatively more important proxy for rural innovation and young entrepreneurship and finally provides some guidelines for how innovation impacts regions differently.

Governments looking to reduce territorial disparities may consider understanding challenges from the point of view of rural communities.

Understanding how to address some of the challenges in rural areas starts with setting the scene but needs to address critical issues that hinder innovation and entrepreneurship because of framework conditions and barriers to interlinkages between regions and abroad.

References

Acemoglu, D. and P. Restrepo (2020), "Robots and jobs: Evidence from US labor markets", *Journal of Political Economy*, Vol. 128/6, pp. 2188-2244, https://doi.org/10.1086/705716. [4]

Akcigit, U., J. Grigsby and T. Nicholas (2017), "The rise of American ingenuity: Innovation and inventors of the golden age", No. w23047, National Bureau of Economic Research. [5]

Aldea-Löppönen, A. (2011), "Social innovation in service delivery to youth in remote and rural areas", *International Journal of Innovation and Regional Development*, pp. 63-81, https://doi.org/10.1504/IJIRD.2011.038063. [15]

Autor, D. (2014), *Polanyi's Paradox and the Shape of Employment Growth*, National Bureau of Economic Research, Cambridge, MA, https://doi.org/10.3386/w20485. [11]

Bekker, V. et al. (2013), "Social innovation in the public sector: an integrative framework", *LIPSE Project Working Articles*, https://www.semanticscholar.org/paper/SOCIAL-INNOVATION-IN-THE-PUBLIC-SECTOR%3A-AN-Bekkers-Tummers/e94141a318649481d4f783aef5dc826f31aa7b9a. [22]

Bock, B. (2016), "Rural marginalisation and the role of social innovation: A turn towards nexogenous development and rural reconnection", *Sociologia Ruralis*, Vol. 56/4, pp. 552–573, https://doi.org/10.1111/soru.12119. [16]

Christmann, G. (2017), "Analysing changes in discursive constructions of rural areas in the context of demographic change: Towards counterpoints in the dominant discourse on "dying villages"", *Comparative Population Studies*, Vol. 41/3-4, pp. 359–378, https://doi.org/10.12765/CPoS-2017-03en. [19]

Dorfmobil Barsikow (2020), *Homepage*, http://dorfmobil.barsikow.de/. [20]

Eurostat (n.d.), *European Union Labour Force Survey (EU-LFS)*, European Union, https://ec.europa.eu/eurostat/web/microdata/european-union-labour-force-survey. [26]

Goos, M., A. Manning and A. Salomons (2014), "Explaining job polarization: Routine-biased technological change and offshoring", *American Economic Review*, Vol. 104/8, pp. 2509-2526, https://doi.org/10.1257/aer.104.8.2509. [7]

Goos, M., A. Manning and A. Salomons (2009), "Job polarization in Europe", *American Economic Review*, Vol. 99/2, pp. 58-63, https://doi.org/10.1257/aer.99.2.58. [6]

Greenan, N. (2003), "Organisational change, technology, employment and skills: an empirical study of French manufacturing", *Cambridge Journal of Economics*, Vol. 27/2, pp. 287-316, https://doi.org/10.1093/cje/27.2.287. [8]

Jungsberg, L. et al. (2020), "Key actors in community-driven social innovation in rural areas in the Nordic countries", *Journal of Rural Studies* 79, pp. 276-285, https://doi.org/10.1016/j.jrurstud.2020.08.004. [23]

Lindberg, M. and A. Jansson (2016), "Regional social innovation – Pinpointing socially inclusive change for smart, inclusive and sustainable growth in European regional development policy", *International Journal of Innovation and Regional Development*, Vol. 7/2, pp. 123-140, https://doi.org/10.1504/IJIRD.2016.077888. [17]

Markey, S., L. Ryser and G. Halseth (2020), "The critical role of services during crisis and recovery: Learning from smarter services and infrastructure projects". [1]

Moulaert, F. et al. (eds.) (2014), *The International Handbook on Social Innovation: Collective Action, Social Learning and Transdisciplinary Research*, Edward Elgar, Cheltenham. [14]

Neumeier, S. (2017), "Social innovation in rural development: Identifying the key factors of success", *Geographical Journal*, Vol. 183/1, https://doi.org/10.1111/geoj.12180. [18]

Noack, A. and T. Federwisch (2020), "Social innovation in rural regions: Older adults and creative community development", *Rural Sociology*, https://doi.org/10.1111/ruso.12333. [25]

OECD (2021), "Building local ecosystems for social innovation: A methodological framework", *OECD Local Economic and Employment Development (LEED) Papers*, No. 2021/06, OECD Publishing, Paris, https://doi.org/10.1787/bef867cd-en. [21]

OECD (2021), *Policies for Present and Future Service Delivery Across Territories*, OECD, Paris. [2]

OECD (2020), "Strengthening online e-learning when schools are closed: The Role of Families and teachers in supporting students during the COVID-19 Crisis", *OECD Policy Responses to Coronavirus (COVID-19)*, OECD, Paris, http://www.oecd.org/coronavirus/policy-responses/strengthening-online-learning-when-schools-are-closed-the-role-of-families-and-teachers-in-supporting-students-during-the-covid-19-crisis-c4ecba6c/. [3]

OECD (2016), *OECD Regional Outlook 2016: Productive Regions for Inclusive Societies*, OECD Publishing, Paris, https://doi.org/10.1787/9789264260245-en. [10]

OECD (2000), *OECD LEED Forum on Social Innovations*, OECD, Paris, https://www.oecd.org/fr/cfe/leed/forum-social-innovations.htm#Definition. [12]

OECD (forthcoming), "Challenges in regional innovation diffusion: A self-assessment toolkit", OECD, Paris. [27]

OECD (forthcoming), *Enhancing Innovation in Rural Regions: Scotland (UK)*, OECD Publishing, Paris. [29]

OECD (n.d.), *OECD Regional Demography (database)*, OECD, Paris, https://stats.oecd.org/Index.aspx?DataSetCode=REGION_DEMOGR. [28]

Richter, R. et al. (2019), *Social Entrepreneurship and Innovation in Rural Europe*, Routledge, New York, https://doi.org/10.4324/9781351038461. [24]

Thesmar, D. and M. Thoenig (2000), "Creative destruction and firm organization choice", *The Quarterly Journal of Economics*, Vol. 115/4, pp. 1201-1237, https://doi.org/10.1162/003355300555051. [9]

Zivojinovic, I., A. Ludvig and K. Hogl (2019), "Social innovation to sustain rural communities: Overcoming institutional challenges in Serbia", *Sustainability*, Vol. 11/24, p. 7248, https://doi.org/10.3390/su11247248. [13]

Notes

[1] A full chapter focused on social innovation in Scotland is explored in OECD (forthcoming[29]), *Enhancing Innovation in Rural Regions: Scotland (UK)*.

[2] Unfortunately, a more precise estimate of patents per patentable occupation was not available for OECD countries on a regional level. The estimates here are therefore based on innovation as measured by patents per working-age labour force participant. Based on the descriptive analysis, we should interpret the estimates based on patents to high-tech occupations as a lower bound estimate. Regions with relatively more rural characteristics are defined as those that have a degree of rurality above the 25th percentile of the index distribution. Controls for this analysis include sectoral and employment shares in sectors, including in mining sectors. The model is a fixed effects regression, which accounts for regional and other time-invariant characteristics. Age groups are excluded, as the regressions already report the elderly dependency ratios which are relatively important for understanding the share of active population.

Annex A. Understanding explained and unexplained differences between two groups through a counter-factual exercise: The Oaxaca-Blinder decomposition

In the early 1970s, Oaxaca and Blinder popularised a framework for decomposing differences between two groups attributed to observable and non-observable characteristics. A typical application of the model is the creation of a counterfactual that divides any observed gap between two exclusive sub-groups into components that are observed as characteristics of individuals and a component that contributes to the difference in the structure of outcome variables (Fortin, Lemieux and Firpo, 2011[1]). Since then, the Oaxaca-Blinder decomposition has been one of the most widely used models for understanding what may be attributed to observable and non-observable characteristics between two groups. A simplified version of their model decomposes intergroup differences in two parts. The decomposition aims to understand what part of the differences in the mean outcomes of each group: $R = E(Y_a) - E(Y_b)$ where Y are expected outcome variables for groups a and b.

We can apply a linear estimation form and model assumptions to the differences between both groups and generate the following for our reference groups A and B:

$$R = \bar{Y}_a - \bar{Y}_b = (\bar{X}_A - \bar{X}_B)'\hat{\beta}_B + \bar{X}'_B(\hat{\beta}_A - \hat{\beta}_B) + (\bar{X}_A - \bar{X}_B)'(\hat{\beta}_A - \hat{\beta}_B)$$

which gives us three components. The first component is the difference between observable predictors ("endowments"). The second part is the difference between coefficients ("coefficients effect"). The last component is the interaction effect, which is the difference simultaneously attributed between the two groups. The coefficients effect is the outcome that measures the expected change in group B's mean outcome if group B had group A's coefficients. If we applied this to male-female wage gaps, the coefficient effect would measure the mean outcome of women, if women had the same attributes as men. The second and third parts of the decomposition are often referred to as the unexplained differences between groups. Most applications of this method have been used to look at differences in gender wage gaps but have also been used for differences between ethnicity, union membership and immigrant status in the labour economics literature. It has also been extended to analysis in gaps in test scores, schools and countries. The decomposition has some similar attributes to the programme evaluation literature, as it generates counterfactual interpretation through the assignment of a "treatment" as the unobservable component of the decomposition, but falls short of fully understanding the mechanisms under which discrimination, or unobserved differences, occurs (Fortin, Lemieux and Firpo, 2011[1]; Jann, 2008[2]; Oaxaca, 1973[3]).

Annex B. Regression analysis on the probability of starting a firm for young entrepreneurs

Table A B.1. Probability of starting a firm for young entrepreneurs, 2019

Young start-up entrepreneurship	(1) All	(2) All	(3) All	(4) All	(5) All	(6) Cities	(7) Towns and suburbs	(8) Rural
Towns and suburbs	-0.073***	-0.055**	-0.048*	-0.049*	-0.038			
	[0.025]	[0.025]	[0.026]	[0.026]	[0.025]			
Rural areas	-0.114***	-0.093***	-0.091***	-0.102***	-0.086***			
	[0.026]	[0.027]	[0.028]	[0.030]	[0.030]			
Female		-0.124***	-0.115***	-0.081***	-0.077***	-0.054*	-0.098***	-0.099**
		[0.019]	[0.021]	[0.020]	[0.021]	[0.029]	[0.029]	[0.044]
Unemployed (last year)		0.774***	0.792***	0.813***	0.808***	0.852***	0.693***	0.867***
		[0.046]	[0.045]	[0.045]	[0.045]	[0.059]	[0.062]	[0.096]
In training (last year)		0.432***	0.420***	0.428***	0.429***	0.534***	0.310***	0.177
		[0.050]	[0.052]	[0.052]	[0.051]	[0.059]	[0.080]	[0.109]
Foreigner			-0.071**	-0.077***	-0.075**	-0.094**	-0.067	0.022
			[0.029]	[0.030]	[0.029]	[0.040]	[0.055]	[0.074]
Secondary education	0.194***	0.234***	0.238***	0.223***	0.225***	0.133***	0.285***	0.305***
	[0.031]	[0.034]	[0.037]	[0.036]	[0.035]	[0.045]	[0.054]	[0.068]
Tertiary education	0.381***	0.447***	0.467***	0.418***	0.420***	0.333***	0.510***	0.451***
	[0.038]	[0.043]	[0.046]	[0.045]	[0.044]	[0.061]	[0.060]	[0.089]
Father's education: primary			-0.006	-0.003	-0.002	-0.045	0.005	0.015
			[0.052]	[0.052]	[0.052]	[0.104]	[0.083]	[0.076]
Father's education: secondary			0.104*	0.110*	0.111**	0.139	0.065	0.138**
			[0.055]	[0.056]	[0.056]	[0.102]	[0.077]	[0.067]
Father's education: tertiary			0.039	0.047	0.042	0.016	0.052	0.113
			[0.059]	[0.060]	[0.060]	[0.108]	[0.091]	[0.112]
Mother's education: primary			-0.044	-0.030	-0.025	-0.139	0.073	0.013
			[0.058]	[0.058]	[0.058]	[0.104]	[0.089]	[0.062]
Mother's education: secondary			0.023	0.039	0.040	-0.008	0.065	0.148**
			[0.049]	[0.049]	[0.049]	[0.098]	[0.067]	[0.063]
Mother's education: tertiary			0.068	0.087	0.088	-0.062	0.293***	0.112
			[0.053]	[0.054]	[0.054]	[0.088]	[0.081]	[0.098]
Work from home				-0.154***	-0.144***	-0.166***	-0.090***	-0.166***
				[0.020]	[0.021]	[0.034]	[0.024]	[0.033]

Young start-up entrepreneurship	(1)	(2)	(3)	(4)	(5)	(6)	(7)	(8)
	All	All	All	All	All	Cities	Towns and suburbs	Rural
Work weekends and nights				0.116***	0.118***	0.135***	0.105**	0.095**
				[0.020]	[0.020]	[0.032]	[0.041]	[0.045]
Looking for a job				0.055	0.052	0.057	-0.014	0.158*
				[0.042]	[0.042]	[0.069]	[0.061]	[0.086]
Constant	-2.719***	-2.793***	-2.769***	-2.569***	-2.723***	-2.610***	-2.977***	-2.994***
	[0.048]	[0.057]	[0.066]	[0.153]	[0.178]	[0.290]	[0.319]	[0.270]
Country fixed effects	Yes	Yes	Yes	Yes	Yes	Yes	Yes	Yes
Socio-economic fixed effects	No	No	Yes	Yes	Yes	Yes	Yes	Yes
Sector fixed effects	No	No	No	No	Yes	Yes	Yes	Yes
Occupation fixed effects	No	No	No	No	Yes	Yes	Yes	Yes
Observations	1 033 674	1 033 674	942 312	939 840	939 430	294 287	349 021	295 814

Note: Reported coefficients are from a probit model with standard errors clustered at a regional level. The reference group for parents' education level are parents who do not live with individuals at home. Robust standard errors in brackets.

*** $p<0.01$, ** $p<0.05$, * $p<0.1$.

Source: Eurostat (n.d.[4]), *European Union Labour Force Survey (EU-LFS)*, https://ec.europa.eu/eurostat/web/microdata/european-union-labour-force-survey.

Annex C. Impact of innovation, by regional characteristics

Table A C.1. Innovation and outcomes in rural versus more densely populated areas, fixed effects regressions on relatively rural regions (>= 75th percentile of degree of rurality)

Impact of ratio of patents to labour force on employment, productivity, household income, growth in value-added per worker and the Gini index, 2000-19

Variable	(1) First-step	(2) Employment (log)	(3) Productivity	(4) Household income (log)	(5) Growth in value-added per work	(6) Gini
Ratio of patents to labour force, per 1 000		**2.099*****	**0.913*****	**0.859*****	**0.220****	**0.111*****
		(0.215)	**(0.244)**	**(0.189)**	**(0.096)**	**(0.010)**
Productivity growth (1y lag)	0.006					
	(0.006)					
HH real income (1y lag)	0.000***					
	(0.000)					
Share of educated workers (1y lag)	0.000					
	(0.000)					
Elderly dependency ratio (1y lag)	0.002***					
	(0.000)					
Population density (1y lag)	-0.000					
	(0.000)					
Population density growth (1y lag)	0.000***					
	(0.000)					
Gender difference in labour market participation rate (1y lag)	-0.014					
	(0.011)					
Constant	-0.035***					
	(0.009)					
Observations	3 768	3 766	3 766	2 929	3 766	3 766
R-squared	0.107	0.440	0.434	0.390	0.204	-0.201
Number of clusters	221	221	221	169	221	221
F-test	60.90	166.4	124.1	86.67	40.48	29.46
Standard errors	Fixed effects	Fixed effects	Fixed effects	Fixed effects	Fixed effects	Fixed effects

Note: Predominantly rural regions refer to regions that are characterised as regions above the 25th percentile of the TL2 rurality index. More densely populated areas are TL2 regions with a degree of rurality that is less than the 25th percentile. Values include linear projections for years with missing values. The first-step estimation model is a fixed effects model on the level of TL2 with lagging independent variables. The second-step estimation includes controls for sectoral employment and value-added per worker. Controls include lags and shares in gross value added and employment in each major NACE sector. Regression is a two-stage least-squared fixed effects model. F-tests are all statistically significant to the 0.001 level. Standard errors are in parentheses.
*** p<0.01, ** p<0.05, * p<0.1.
Source: OECD Regional Demography (database) (OECD[5]).

Table A C.2. Innovation and outcomes in rural versus more densely populated areas, fixed effects regression on more densely populated regions (< 25th percentile of degree of rurality)

Impact of ratio of patents to labour force on employment, productivity, household income, growth in value-added per worker and the Gini index, 2000-19

	(7)	(8)	(9)	(10)	(11)	(12)
Variables	First-step	Employment (log)	Productivity	HH income (log)	Growth in VAPW	Gini
Ratio of patents to labour force, per 1 000		0.380***	0.539***	0.296*	0.126**	0.027***
		(0.094)	(0.140)	(0.156)	(0.059)	(0.007)
Productivity growth (1y lag)	0.019					
	(0.043)					
HH real income (1y lag)	0.000***					
	(0.000)					
Share of educated workers (1y lag)	0.000					
	(0.001)					
Elderly dependency ratio (1y lag)	0.002**					
	(0.001)					
Population density (1y lag)	0.000***					
	(0.000)					
Population density growth (1y lag)	-0.000					
	(0.000)					
Gender difference in LM participation rate (1y lag)						
Constant	-0.018					
	(0.029)					
Observations	1 271	1 271	1 271	1 231	1 271	1 271
R-squared	0.099	0.604	0.367	0.446	0.151	0.175
Number of clusters	80	80	80	70	80	80
F-test	21.59	83.41	35.67	41.89	11.18	17.27
Standard errors	Fixed effects	Fixed effects	Fixed effects	Fixed effects	Fixed effects	Fixed effects

Note: Predominantly rural regions refer to regions that are characterised as regions above the 25th percentile of the TL2 rurality index. More densely populated areas are TL2 regions with a degree of rurality that is less than the 25th percentile. Values include linear projections for years with missing values. The first-step estimation model is a fixed effects model on the level of TL2 with lagging independent variables. The second-step estimation includes controls for sectoral employment and value-added per worker. Controls include lags and shares in gross value added and employment in each major NACE sector. Regression is a two-stage least-squared fixed effects model. F-tests are all statistically significant to the 0.001 level. Standard errors are in parentheses.
*** p<0.01, ** p<0.05, * p<0.1.
Source: OECD Regional Demography (database) (OECD[5]).

Annex D. Patentable occupations

The proposal on adjusting innovation indicators for the occupational structure or rural economies comes from discussions with the OECD Expert Advisory Committee for Rural Innovation. During the sessions, several rural academics identified structural problems associated with how innovation is measured in rural areas and why the bias associated may not be territorially homogenous. To address this, work by Dotzel (2017[6]) and Wojan (2021[7]) proposes an occupation-driven approach for analysing regional invention. The authors argue that patenting rates should be computed on the subset of workers that might plausibly contribute to patenting. To do this, the authors regress the aggregate number of patents produced in the commuting zone during the period 2000-05 on the share of the workforce employed in a selection of detailed census occupations. The authors' commuting zone-level regression includes controls on the patent stock, human capital share (working-age population with a bachelor's degree or higher), population density, a natural amenity score and the wage-rental ratio. They apply the analysis to a core set of occupations (from the U.S. Department of Labor Employment and Training Administration O*NET database) defined by the National Science Foundation's classification of science, engineering and technical (SET) occupations, along with an iterative random selection of other occupations that may have a strong association with patenting. Ten thousand regressions are estimated with 19 non-SET occupations randomly included in each estimation. The inventive subset inclusion criteria for the non-SET occupations are those occupations-associated coefficients that are positive and significant in at least 75% of their regressions in the metro or non-metro analysis and are characterised as inventive. Of the 300 non-SET occupations included in the analysis, 11 are identified as inventive, that is consistently associated with positive, significant coefficients.

Table A D.1 provides a list of occupations with a relatively high probability of patent. Furthermore, Figure A D.1. demonstrate the distribution of these occupations as a share of the total employed population (patent intensity) across the United States. As demonstrated in Figure 3.4, adjusting for these shares reduces disparities in patenting intensities between territories. In comparison, patent intensity over total employment, over just knowledge-intensive or high-tech sectors provided in Figure A D.2. Adjusting denominators in patenting intensity (TL2), descriptively points towards the same direction, but statistically does not provide as powerful an argument. This could be due to loss of precision in TL2 level aggregation and relevance of the occupations included.

Table A D.1. Inventive occupations

Occupations with a high (>75%) probability to patent

Census code(s)	Occupation
100-176, 190-196	Science, engineering, and technical (SET) occupations
005	Marketing and sales managers
030	Engineering managers
181	Market and survey researchers
263	Designers
284	Technical writers
772	Electrical, electronics and electromechanical assemblers
790	Computer control programmers and operators
803	Machinists
806	Model makers and patternmakers, metal and plastic
813	Tool and die makers
884	Semiconductor processors

Note: Occupations associated with coefficients that are positive and significant in at least 75% of their regressions in the metro or non-metro analysis are characterised as inventive.
Source: Dotzel, K. (2017[6]), "Three essays on human capital and innovation in the United States", Chapter 3, Graduate School of the Ohio State University; Wojan, T. (2021[7]), "An occupational approach for analyzing regional invention", National Center for Science and Engineering Statistics, https://ncses.nsf.gov/pubs/ncses22202/assets/ncses22202.pdf.

Figure A D.1. Inventive occupations in the US

Shares on the county level

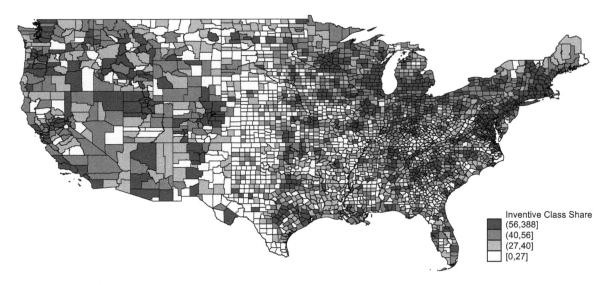

Note: Shares represent the shares of occupations likely to be patented as a part of all employed labour defined in Wojan (2021[7]).
Source: U.S. Census Bureau.

Figure A D.2. Adjusting denominators in patenting intensity (TL2)

Information and communication technology (ICT) patents to employment in knowledge-intensive and high-tech sectors (adjusted) ratios versus ICT patents to active labour force (15-64 year-olds) in OECD countries, 2019

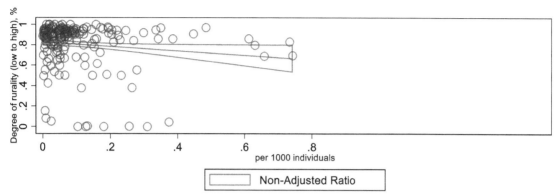

A linear OLS regression estimate on the correlation between non-adjusted patent ratios and degree of rurality is .0014, but not-significantly different from 0 with a p-value of .973.

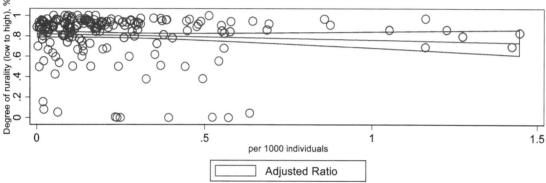

A linear OLS regression estimate of the correlation between adjusted patent ratios and degree of rurality is -.0008, but not-significantly different from 0 with a p-value of .99.

Note: The numerator in the ratios is the total number of patents in ICT per TL2 region. The denominator in the non-adjusted values is the total active labour force (15-64 year-olds). The denominator in the adjusted values is employment in knowledge-intensive sectors. The denominator in the non-adjusted ratios. The degree of rurality on the y-axis captures the percentage of individuals living in non-metropolitan regions within the TL2 regions. For visual purposes, outliers in degree of rurality and the respective ratios are omitted. Linear extrapolation was used for TL2 regions with missing values in 2019. Regression output on the correlation between each of the ratios and the degree of rurality for the reference year, 2019, includes country controls and lagged controls on productivity, real household income, education shares, elderly dependency ratios, population density, population growth and population gender differences.
Source: European Patent Office (PATSTAT[8]), OECD Regional Demography (database) (OECD[5]).

Annex E. European national innovation trends

Innovation trends using the EU Community Innovation Survey and national percentages of rural populations

More general trends in non-patent-related innovations are explored using the EU Community Innovation Survey's most recent iteration in 2014. Because of the lack of availability of data on a subnational level, all analysis is conducted on a national level, splitting countries with relative shares of rural populations. This limitation does not permit a full territorial analysis using self-reported measures of innovation; however, it provides a general outlook of what is observed on the aggregate level.

Most firms do not innovate but when they do, they tend to have innovations that are new to the firm but not necessarily to the market. When firms do innovate, most innovations are introductions of new products or processes into the production cycle of the firm. In comparison, only 9% of firms introduce new innovations to the market (Figure A E.1).

Figure A E.1. Innovators, 2014

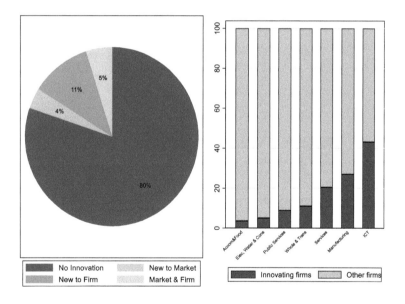

Note: Data is from the last available year. OECD countries with available data include the Czech Republic, Estonia, Germany, Greece, Hungary, Latvia, Lithuania, Norway, Portugal, the Slovak Republic and Spain. In this figure, predominantly rural refers to areas that have a rural population that is above the 25th percentile of the distribution of country-specific shares of the rural population. In this case, this refers to countries that have more than approximately 20% of the population in rural regions. This relatively low threshold accommodates countries that have an important share of the population in rural regions but are not primarily rural. Estimates from the survey are weighted averages.
Source: Eurostat (n.d.[9]), *Community Innovation Survey (CIS)*, https://ec.europa.eu/eurostat/web/microdata/community-innovation-survey, data from 2014.

While more innovations occur in the manufacturing sector, the share of total innovative firms within each sector is higher for ICT firms (Figure A E.2). In countries with relatively larger rural populations, innovative ICT and manufacturing sectors have relatively higher shares of the economy as compared to countries with a very low share of the rural population. The evidence demonstrated is in line with the observations on the sectoral component of innovation. Manufacturing firms have a production cycle that may more easily incorporate changes, whereas long-standing and traditional industries that dominate much of the economy in rural regions may not necessarily have the same demand for innovation.

Interestingly, in areas with a relatively higher share of rural populations, there is a higher share of innovative firms that provide public services such as education, health, community services and public administrative support services. To some extent, this may reflect different types of entrepreneurship that have a social purpose.

Figure A E.2. Innovators and shares

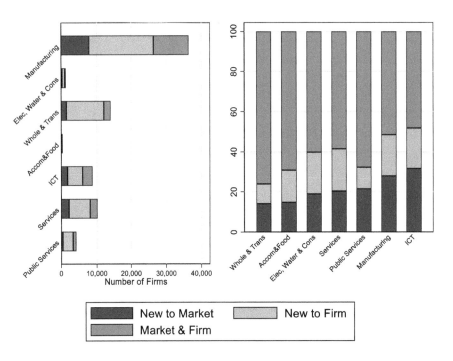

Note: OECD countries with available data include the Czech Republic, Estonia, Germany, Greece, Hungary, Latvia, Lithuania, Norway, Portugal, the Slovak Republic and Spain. In this figure, predominantly rural refers to areas that have a rural population that is above the 25th percentile of the distribution of country-specific shares of the rural population. In this case, this refers to countries that have more than approximately 20% of rural populations. This relatively low threshold accommodates countries that have an important share of the population in rural regions but are not primarily rural. Estimates from the survey are weighted averages.
Source: Eurostat (n.d.[9]), *Community Innovation Survey (CIS)*, https://ec.europa.eu/eurostat/web/microdata/community-innovation-survey, data from 2014.

Innovation is associated with high-growth firms, however, on a country level, the trend is not linear.[1] In Figure A E.3, the association between the share of the rural population and the average growth in turnover for innovating firms is positive. Analysing the characteristics of high-growth firms is insightful for understanding longer-term payoffs from innovation and its adoption and diffusion in competitive settings. Data from European countries show that the sectors with the highest share of high-growth firms are in the ICT and services sector[2] while Figure A E.4 also demonstrates that many of the countries with high shares of innovative ICT and manufacturing sectors are located in economies with larger rural shares.

Figure A E.3. High growth and rural populations, 2014

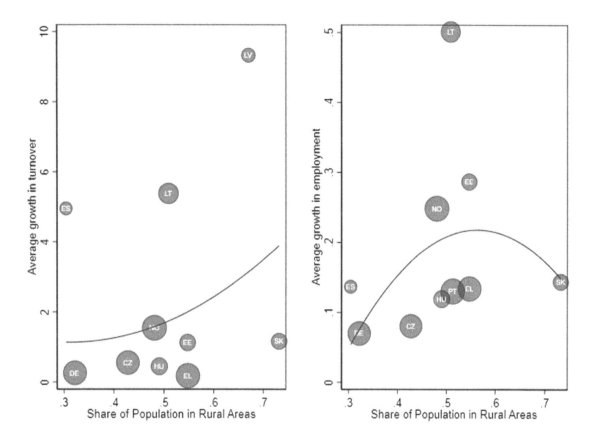

Note: High growth in turnover refers to firms in the top quartile of change in turnover within each sector and country. High employment growth refers to firms in the top quartile of change in employment within each sector and country. OECD countries with available data include the Czech Republic, Estonia, Germany, Greece, Hungary, Latvia, Lithuania, Norway, Portugal, the Slovak Republic and Spain.

Source: Eurostat (n.d.[9]), *Community Innovation Survey (CIS)*, https://ec.europa.eu/eurostat/web/microdata/community-innovation-survey, data from 2014.

Figure A E.4. Share high-growth firms and innovators, 2014

Note: High growth refers to firms in the top quartile of change in turnover within each sector and country. OECD countries with available data include the Czech Republic, Estonia, Germany, Greece, Hungary, Latvia, Lithuania, Norway, Portugal, the Slovak Republic and Spain. In this figure, predominantly rural refers to areas that have a rural population that is above the 25th percentile of the distribution of country-specific shares of the rural population. In this case, this refers to countries that have more than approximately 20% of rural populations. This relatively low threshold accommodates countries that have an important share of the population in rural regions but are not primarily rural.
Source: Eurostat (n.d.[9]), *Community Innovation Survey (CIS)*, https://ec.europa.eu/eurostat/web/microdata/community-innovation-survey, data from 2014.

Notes

[1] According to the data from the EU Community Innovation Survey, there is no significant correlation between innovation undertaken and higher firm growth in the same year. There is moreover no data available for understanding if innovation is correlated with high growth in subsequent years. In this simple regression, controls were included for percentage of rural populations within countries and country and sector fixed effects.

[2] High-growth firms are defined as firms with growth in the top quartile of firm turnover in the distribution of firms within each country and sector.

Annex F. Creative occupations in the US

Figure A F.1. Creative occupations in the US

Share of creative sectors, by county level

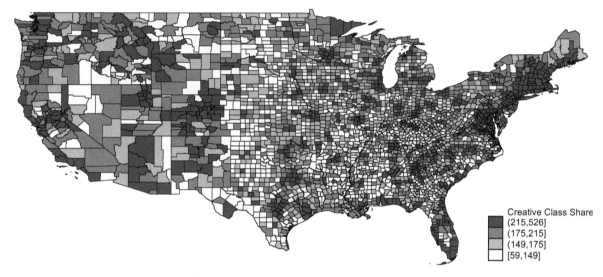

Creative Class Share
(215,526]
(175,215]
(149,175]
[59,149]

Note: The figure represents the share of employment in creative occupations overall employment, per 1 000 employed workers. Occupations considered creative are identified through O*NET classification of occupations and were described as "thinking creatively" following the method set up by Florida (2002[10]) and the US Department for Agriculture's Economic Research Service (2020[11]).
Source: Florida, R. (2002[10]), *The Rise of the Creative Class*, Basic Books, New York; USDA ERS (2020[11]), *Documentation*, https://www.ers.usda.gov/data-products/creative-class-county-codes/documentation/ (accessed on 3 November 2021); U.S. Census Bureau.

References

Dotzel, K. (2017), "Three essays on human capital and innovation in the United States", Chapter 3, Graduate School of the Ohio State University. [6]

Eurostat (n.d.), *Community Innovation Survey (CIS)*, https://ec.europa.eu/eurostat/web/microdata/community-innovation-survey. [9]

Eurostat (n.d.), *European Union Labour Force Survey (EU-LFS)*, European Union, https://ec.europa.eu/eurostat/web/microdata/european-union-labour-force-survey. [4]

Florida, R. (2002), *The Rise of the Creative Class*, Basic Books, New York. [10]

Fortin, N., T. Lemieux and S. Firpo (2011), "Decomposition methods in economics", in *Handbook of Labor Economics*, Elsevier, https://doi.org/10.1016/s0169-7218(11)00407-2. [1]

Jann, B. (2008), "The Blinder–Oaxaca decomposition for linear regression models", *The Stata Journal: Promoting Communications on Statistics and Stata*, Vol. 8/4, pp. 453-479, https://doi.org/10.1177/1536867x0800800401.   [2]

Oaxaca, R. (1973), "Male-female wage differentials in urban labor markets", *International Economic Review*, Vol. 14/3, pp. 693-709, https://www.jstor.org/stable/2525981 (accessed on 2 December 2020).   [3]

OECD (n.d.), *OECD Regional Demography (database)*, OECD, Paris, https://stats.oecd.org/Index.aspx?DataSetCode=REGION_DEMOGR.   [5]

PATSTAT (n.d.), *European Patent Office*, https://www.epo.org/searching-for-patents/business/patstat.html (accessed on 2021).   [8]

USDA ERS (2020), *Documentation*, U.S. Department of Agriculture Economic Research Service, https://www.ers.usda.gov/data-products/creative-class-county-codes/documentation/ (accessed on 3 November 2021).   [11]

Wojan, T. (2021), "An occupational approach for analyzing regional invention", National Center for Science and Engineering Statistics, https://ncses.nsf.gov/pubs/ncses22202/assets/ncses22202.pdf.   [7]

CPSIA information can be obtained
at www.ICGtesting.com
Printed in the USA
BVHW021259141022
649460BV00020B/1158